Car Living When There's No Other Choice:
Tips & Strategies for Survival & Safety

Veronica Harnish

Liraji Media • Ashland, Oregon • U.S.A.

Cover photo: Veronica Harnish. Cover design by Susan Veach <www.susanveach.com>
Contact email: carlivingbook@gmx.com

Liraji Media, Oregon, USA
International Standard Book Number/ISBN-13: 978-0615779744
ISBN-10: 0615779743
Produced and distributed in the United States of America
Library of Congress Control Number: 2013933897
Harnish, Veronica
Car Living When There's No Other Choice/by Veronica Harnish.
ISBN: (Book) 978-0615779744 (Liraji Media)
Update Codes: EKEJR3847DJSFK; 54KDNEOR927; 2146EIWNV39; 845JSLDF754; 253DSO

First Edition/Version 1.0— 04/2013

Warning Disclaimer:
The purpose of this book is to educate, entertain, and provide accurate information with regard to the subject matter covered. However, the author and publisher accept no responsibility or liability for inaccuracies or omissions. The author and the publisher specifically disclaim any liability, loss, or risk, whether personal, financial or otherwise, that is incurred as a consequence, directly or indirectly, from the use and/or application of any of the contents of this book.

This book is designed to provide information on car living, and is sold with the understanding that the publisher and author are not engaged in rendering legal, medical, accounting or other professional services. If legal or other expert assistance is required, the services of a competent professional should be sought.

Every effort has been made to make this book as complete and as accurate as possible. However, there *may be mistakes*, both typographical and in content. Therefore, this text should be used only as a general guide and not as the ultimate source of car living information. Further, this book contains information on car living that is current only up to the printing date.

The author and publisher shall have neither liability nor responsibility to any person or entity with respect to any loss or damage caused, or alleged to have been caused, directly or indirectly, by the information contained in this book. If you do not wish to be bound by the above, you may return this book to the publisher for a full refund.

Product Disclaimer:
Reference herein to any specific commercial products, process, or service by trade name, trademark, manufacturer, or otherwise, is provided for information and example purposes only, and does not necessarily constitute or imply its endorsement, recommendation, or favoring by the author or publisher.

For Violet Ellen Phillips,
a 67-year-old homeless woman set on fire
while she slept on a bus bench in Van Nuys, California*

For everyone who has helped someone else not to have to live in a car. – Steve Fenwick

To all those of us who have had to take one step backwards in order to later be able to take two forward. Know that better days will come. – Louis Lipp

To Charlotte and Brenda, who always make sure there's love and help for those who are in need. – Joe Borecki

In memory of Josephine Hartz and Vivian Hipsley, who were 'liberated ladies' decades before the term was invented. – Margaret (Peggy-Price) Hartz

* http://articles.latimes.com/2013/jan/20/local/la-me-homeless-fire-20130120

"When I go to sleep in my car,
it feels good knowing I helped save all those banks."

—bumpersticker by Duck and Cover of Oakland, CA
http://www.duckandcoverprod.com

CONTENTS

INTRODUCTION

Car living is the polite term for what you really are—homeless—regardless of whether you choose to live in a vehicle, or were forced into the situation unwillingly. The federal Housing and Urban Development (HUD) agency defines a homeless person as "a person sleeping in a place *not meant for human habitation* [emphasis mine] or in an emergency shelter; and a person in transitional housing for homeless persons who originally came from the street or an emergency shelter."[1]

These days, there are so many different ways to get down on your luck or become homeless, and so few means to escape. It is much harder to climb out of the hole of homelessness than it is to fall in. To be homeless is to be a pariah in a society where a person's bank balance, rather than their humanity, determines their level of respectability.

Car living is hardly a lifestyle choice—it's a last-ditch effort to survive and stay off the streets. Some people are loners and have no support system, such as family, to help. Others aren't loners, and have a wide circle of friends and family, who either can't or won't help. If you end up living in your vehicle (or are on the verge of it), you probably have nowhere else to go, otherwise friends and family would have taken you in. Car living is a step up from street homelessness, but is not much safer. Car dwellers have been beaten, robbed, raped, stabbed and shot, just like people who live on the streets.[2] The average age of death of a homeless person is 47. They are 13 times more likely to be the victims of violence than a housed person.[3]

In today's economy, with the record number of foreclosures and high unemployment, car living is more of a last resort than a bohemian or vagabond lifestyle choice some people prefer to live. This book does not teach how to live in a car long-term, or as a permanent lifestyle. It's also not about living in a vehicle for a couple of weeks on a road trip, where you know you have a home to return to after your trip is over. You will encounter many of the same problems whether you choose to live in your car willingly or not. It's one thing to live in your vehicle because you love a freewheeling lifestyle; it's quite another to do it when you have nowhere else to go. Unlike vagabonding, involuntary homelessness is enforced (eviction, etc.) very stressful, and doesn't have a defined end. This book is about the perpetual "What's going to happen to me next?" anxiety that gnaws at you until the situation resolves. There are a million things that can go wrong, and so few that can go right.

Unlike other car living books, this texts point you *to* available government services, because you paid taxes into the system during your working life to fund those services. Now, as a car dweller, you're merely withdrawing, like a savings account, a fraction of what you put in over those years. Unfortunately, politics will be a major factor as to what help and services are available in your particular area. Anti-government, conservative states never met a social service program whose funding they weren't happy to slash to the bone, while progressive states and cities can be unbelievably generous in providing help. If push comes to shove in your situation, seriously consider traveling to a progressive area if you can while car living, so you can have a more supportive climate and safety net.

It also may be helpful to leave large, expensive cities for places that have a lower cost of living, even for a little while, until you can get back on your feet. Conversely, since rural areas generally have a lot less infrastructure (such as food banks and shelters) than small cities, it may be in your best interest, especially if you are unemployed and not attached to a particular area, to move to a larger location where more services are available. At the very least, try to be within driving distance of towns with services and a reasonable amount of employment opportunities.

The purpose of this book is two-fold: To give you immediate guidance, help, and resources to get you through your current situation, while providing information to wipe out the core issues of homelessness through policy changes. This book addresses the many different scenarios inherent to car living, while giving you a foundation to deal with all of the random variables you will face that can't be covered or anticipated in advance. It's about how to think your way through each situation by noticing what resources are available or acquirable. With each passing month of car dwelling, you won't need a book—you'll get the hang of things and have other circumstances arise in which you'll know exactly what to do, or at the very least, know how to think your way through things.

Following the information in this book isn't foolproof by any means—you could still become a crime victim, and things can still go wrong, despite taking every possible precaution. You are still a vulnerable member of the population. Although this book is no guarantee of safety, it is designed to greatly increase your chances of it.

This book is absolutely not intended as any kind of inspiration. On the contrary, it is a canary in the coal mine, warning that if our political leaders at all levels don't address the core causes of homelessness—and they won't, unless enough of us force them to—more and more people will end up living in vehicles—or worse. There's nothing inspiring about that possibility at all.

Veronica Harnish
April, 2013

1.   WHO ARE THE CAR-DWELLING HOMELESS?

Almost one-third of Seattle's homeless are living in vehicles, of which sixty percent are couples, and eighty percent have a cat or a dog.[4] People with pets often choose to live in cars because most homeless shelters do not allow pets. Also, many shelters only accept married couples or single parents with children. Women's and men's shelters, respectively, allow only women or only men—it doesn't matter if the person is in a relationship.[5]

Lack of affordable housing has been identified as the most common reason for homelessness by the U.S. Conference of Mayors since 2008.[6] More than fifty percent of homeless people work, but do not earn enough to pay for housing.[7] So lack of affordable housing, and the lack of a living wage are the primary causes of the majority of homelessness.

Homelessness, and it's constant companion, poverty, no longer belong almost exclusively to the stereotypical crazy street person, or wino. Only twenty percent of homeless people (known as the "chronic" homeless) are in that situation due to longtime substance abuse or mental illness.[8] Also within that twenty percent bracket are the few people who live in a vehicle as a lifestyle choice.[9] So what about the other eighty percent? Who are they?

The eighty percent are the economic homeless, who are newly displaced by layoffs, foreclosures, or other financial troubles caused by the recession, as well as regressive economic policies such as deregulation and outsourcing. They are people who fall off the economic ladder, whether via a bad economy, unemployment benefits that inevitably run out, or medical bills that bankrupt them. They are veterans or domestic violence victims. They are the people, such as unmarried pregnant women, that shelter workers tell to go camp in the woods because the shelters are full.[10] They are homeless families with children, camped out in cars, tents or motel rooms in Florida.[11] They are people trying to survive on minimum wage jobs, struggling to raise families. They are the working poor, foreclosure victims, the unemployed, the underemployed, youth, and people living in rural areas. They are people living in motels, campgrounds, shelters, storage facilities, parks, public spaces, dumpsters, under freeway overpasses, in abandoned buildings, and in bus, subway or train stations.

Or cars.

But the irony is that the so-called "chronic" homeless, who have substance abuse or mental health issues, are the most visible, even though they make up only twenty percent of the homeless population. You see them panhandling on street corners, sitting in parks with a shopping cart full of belongings, or sleeping on the street or in other public places. The eighty percent majority of the homeless (including car dwellers) are virtually invisible, because they have to be to survive. They can't tip off current (and future) employers, law enforcement, child protective services, potential landlords, or anyone else to their plight.

2. WHAT TO DO BEFORE LIVING IN YOUR CAR

If you have to give up a home to foreclosure or eviction, and can somehow escape with enough cash to rent a room, stationary RV, or mobile home; or if you can stay with family or friends, do so. The ultimate goal is to try to avoid living in your car at all costs to begin with. Car living is a last resort when all other viable options have failed. If you are not homeless yet, it may be possible to avoid becoming homeless by finding out if there are any prevention or emergency assistance programs in your area. Often these programs can help in paying rent, utilities, or bills. If you are homeless now, emergency assistance programs may help with temporary shelter, or security deposits and/or first month's rent.[12]

When homelessness strikes, friends and relatives are often the first place of refuge. If you want to find out who your true friends in life are, tell them you're broke and homeless. Then watch their reaction. Here's a very typical example of what you will encounter, from a man who lived in his car in Los Angeles:

> "I'll be honest, before I became homeless I knew very little about homeless people. While I gave them money occasionally, I was really ignorant about their situation. Why were they homeless? Didn't they have any friends or family to help them? Well, I had 'friends' and I was homeless.

The worst part about being homeless wasn't living on the streets or being hungry; it was having my friends, or the people I thought were my friends, turn their backs on me.

When I called these people they treated my situation with absolutely no urgency. It was as if I told them I just 'had a cold,' and it was no big deal. What was really amazing is many of them would tell me how hard *they* had it. These people were living in houses, condos, and apartments, and would actually tell me their sob stories while I paid for the phone call! Here were some of my friends' reactions:

> "Is this being homeless a comedy routine? No, I can't help."
> "So, why are you callin' me?"
> "Please never contact me again."
> "Wish I could help; I'm in exactly the same boat as you. I'm getting killed in the stock market."
> "Yeah, well, I gotta go, bye!"
> "Wow, sorry to hear times are so tough for you (expletive) (expletive) (expletive)."
> "(Expletive) (expletive) I'll pray for you."
> My parents' reaction: "We're not going to help, but please keep in touch, we sure are thinkin' about you!"

Out of desperation I even called the church I had gone to for many years. This was the same church Ronald Reagan went to for decades, so you would think these wonderful Americans would help, right? Even though I had given them money over the years to build their newest sanctuary, they were not about to help me when I was homeless...Not all churches are like that. Many churches go out of their way to help the poor. If your church, synagogue, or house of worship doesn't help the homeless, ask them why."[13]

So if your friends and family recoil in horror, and slowly back away from you as if you are carrying a highly contagious disease, forget about asking them for help. If they show concern and offer to help—short of being able to to give you a roof over your head—take them up on it. It will save you a lot of money on small but necessary expenses, such as laundry bills, storage unit fees, mailbox fees, etc.

Do not be too proud to ask for help, as there is absolutely no reward in suffering and being miserable. Even the Native Americans had mercy on the pilgrims, and helped save them from starvation.

Below is a brief checklist of steps to take if you're on the verge of living in your car.[14] They are covered in much greater detail throughout the book:

- Find people or organizations who may be willing to help. This includes government social service agencies, family, friends, churches or private foundations. If you can find someone to loan you money, now is the time to ask.
- Think of things you can sell, and services you can eliminate (cable TV, etc.) that can provide cash for emergency funds if homelessness is inevitable.
- If you lost your job, apply for unemployment benefits, even if you think you are ineligible.
- Apply for public and Section 8 housing. Also apply for transitional housing.
- Make sure your ID is current, and that you have a place to receive mail. If you don't have a drivers license, apply for a state ID card instead. If you need a replacement Social Security card sent to you, apply for one. (See Appendix A)
- Pack only what you'll need to live on, and put the rest in storage, or ask a friend or relative to store a few things for you.

Finding Help In Your Area With One Call Or Click

Immediately contact your state, county and local health and human services offices, or the United Way Helpline to see what help is available in your area. You can do this by calling 2-1-1, or visiting http://www.211.org and entering your ZIP code. A United Way service, 2-1-1 provides free and confidential information and referrals for help with food, rent, housing, utilities, employment, health care, counseling, legal assistance and more. This one-stop shopping hotline consolidates government, nonprofit, and faith-based social services so you don't have to make multiple phone calls trying to navigate through a confusing tangle of help agencies and bureaucracy.[15]

Visit the Homelessness Resource Center site if 2-1-1 service is not available in your area (http://homeless.samhsa.gov/Resource/LocalResources.aspx), and click on your state. By making contact with your state agency, they will be able to further refer you to local resources in your specific city. Also visit http://portal.hud.gov/hudportal/HUD?src=/states and click on your state. Then click on "Find Homeless Resources." There, you will find help for shelter, hotlines, utility bill help, food bank locations, Social Security offices, homeless veterans contacts, United Way services, job retraining, and other little-known assistance programs you may qualify for.

If you don't have access to the Internet, most local social service agencies publish "essential services" resource lists of where to find the following in your area:

- At-Risk Youth
- Clothing
- Crisis Intervention
- Debt Counseling and Renegotiation
- Disability Services
- Food
- Free Health Care Clinics & Services

- Legal Assistance
- Rent Subsidy Programs
- Transportation
- Shelter
- Utility Assistance
- Unemployment Benefits
- Veterans Services
- Work Referrals & Job Retraining

You may be eligible for benefits such as unemployment, food stamps, etc., and local service agencies will be able to provide you with lists and referrals to shelters and transitional or subsidized housing. Homeless families tend to get priority in shelters and for government services, such as housing assistance. This is especially true if you have children, because additional assistance, such as cash and motel vouchers, are available under the federal program called Temporary Assistance for Needy Families (TANF).

Do not feel you are taking government "handouts." Your state and federal tax dollars pay for these services, and you are withdrawing a fraction of what you have paid into the system over the course of your working life. This is even moreso if you are working while homeless, so you may as well use what you have already paid for.

If you feel that a homeless shelter is a safer and more viable option than living in your car, or if you want a temporary respite from car dwelling during extreme weather, you can find state-by-state shelter directories at:

- http://www.homelessshelterdirectory.org and
- http://www.shelterlistings.org/find_shelter.html

Specific groups of people are especially vulnerable to homelessness, and have no other choice but to live in their cars. They include veterans, domestic violence victims, youths, people who live in rural areas, and the chronically homeless. There are additional assistance programs and services available to these groups, on top of regular homelessness programs; see Appendix B in the back of this book.

Planning Ahead

Eating, sleeping, going to the bathroom, and storing food, water, and clothing are the primary things you'll do in your car. The rest of the time you'll be outside the vehicle, either working or looking for work, at the gym, grocery shopping, eating, etc. The more advance planning and preparation you can do, the less stressful your car living will be.

Not preparing to live out of your car is like a hiker going out into the wilderness without a backpack full of provisions. If you see the handwriting on the wall that homelessness is imminent, don't go into denial—start preparing immediately. You want to have as much done as possible *before* homelessness hits, because once it does, basic survival becomes an exhausting, full-time job.

The checklists in Appendix C in the back of this book may seem daunting at first, but you already have most of the items listed on hand. It will be much cheaper and time-saving to organize and pack ahead of time, than to try to find these items while on the road. Try to get as much of a head start as possible; if you're in a rush, it can all be done in three days or less, since most of what you're taking you'll already have, or can be purchased in mostly one location, such as dollar stores. They are a life saver for car dwellers, because you can buy miscellaneous necessities and toiletries there for a fraction of what you would pay in a grocery, drug, or convenience store.

Don't be overwhelmed. Pack a little at a time if you don't have to live in your car immediately. When in doubt, keep it simple. And know that even with the best of planning, you'll have to make adjustments to changing circumstances. You can handle them.

Living in a car in many ways is similar to disaster preparedness and survival—life is enormously disrupted and uncomfortable for awhile until things return to as close to normal as possible. As a car dweller, you will be living without the same amenities that disaster victims also do without. In addition to the lists in Appendix C, familiarize yourself with what you'll need from the FEMA disaster preparedness checklist, and make adjustments and modifications based on your specific circumstances.[16] For example, if you will be near a reliable water source, or can store a couple of gallon jugs of water in your car on a regular basis, you won't need disaster water packets that are good for eight years.

To begin, start gathering things you already have on hand, such as pillows, blankets, food, clothes and toiletries. Then look at long-term needs, such as a place to shower and a place to store your belongings that won't fit in the car. How much is a gym membership in your area? Or storage unit fees? If you can't afford either, what other possibilities do you have? Can friends or family give you a place to clean up a couple of days a week, or store a few boxes?

Then move on to the particular: Can you use an improvised toilet, such as a lidded bucket with cat litter inside, or do you want to spend roughly $25, plus shipping, for a camping toilet, such as a Luggable Loo or Hassock Portable Lightweight Self-Contained Toilet? Do you need a propane heater in the dead of winter, and if so, what type can you afford? The more money you have to spend on equipment such as a camping cook stove, or a heated blanket that plugs into your cigarette lighter, the less uncomfortable you'll be. Make a budget so you can discern needs from wants.

Prepare at least three outfits for job interviews (in case you are called back for second and third interviews) and place them in a plastic hanging clothes bag. Failing that, poke a small hole in the bottom middle of a black trash bag, just wide enough for the hanger tops to pass through, and use the trash bag as the protective plastic wrap. You can tie a knot in the bottom to seal the clothes in the bag. Store these outfits in your storage unit or your gym locker to keep them from getting smelly or wrinkled in your car.

Some homeless-friendly cities have "day shelters" run by charities where you can do laundry for free, get bus passes, or enjoy a hot meal. (Be aware that many of them require ID and a background check, which they run on the spot when they register you.) See what's available in your area.

Finally, ask yourself this: Where are you going to park and sleep the first night? Start scouting if you can't come up with an immediate answer.

And most important of all, try to spend one or two nights sleeping in the car in your driveway while you still have a home. This way you can make adjustments to cargo space and sleeping configurations *before* it becomes critical and you're under duress. (I was too sick from the flu at the time I became homeless to do this. As a result, due to a low-quality sleeping bag and not enough blankets, I froze the first night I lived in my car when the temperature dropped to 37 degrees.)

3.   CAR LIVING BASICS

Most people don't think of it this way, but a car is like a metal tent. It is an excellent, high-grade form of shelter. It is wind and waterproof, giving you a huge advantage over someone camping in a tent. Unfortunately, like a tent, a car it is not insulated, so while your vehicle will easily protect you from wind and rain, it won't protect you from extreme temperatures.

Most car living books assume you have time and money to optimize your vehicle (i.e., installing insulation, extra car batteries for power, retrofitting, etc.); this book shows you how to work with what you have. A van or RV is great if you have one, as they are practically moveable apartments. However, most people have older sedans or SUVs they'll need to adjust to living inside. One woman in southern California lived in a Volkswagen Beetle with her cat for 18 months![17] Any kind of vehicle as shelter is still better than sleeping in a doorway or dumpster. And if you are an outdoors enthusiast of any kind, you will already be familiar with roughing it.

When living in a car, you have to be extra vigilant, since safety and survival will be your two highest priorities, period. You'll also have to be as invisible and inconspicuous as possible by learning how to hide in plain sight. You will know you're doing things right if no one knows or notices you are homeless.

The most fundamental commandment of homelessness to remember is this: If you look like a homeless person, you will be treated like one.

Hygiene is the primary indicator that you are homeless. As one former car dweller stated:

> "When I was homeless, the first question people would ask me was not, 'Are you hungry?' 'Do you need a place to stay?' 'Do you need a doctor?' Amazingly, it was always, 'Where do you bathe?' I guess they were concerned that if I died in a gutter, my carcass would be nice and clean."[18]

The cold, hard reality is that if you look (and smell) destitute, people will not help you. Conversely, if they see you making a mighty, struggling effort, a few will go out of their way to help you.

Creating Privacy Inside Your Vehicle

If you can afford to have your vehicle windows tinted to the darkest level legally permitted in your state, do so. If not, you can purchase removable, static cling window tint film to use on the side and rear windows. Keep in mind that while window tinting will give you privacy during the day, and keep the car a couple degrees cooler on sunny days, at night you will have difficulty seeing outside. If that is going to pose a security risk for your particular location, use removable window covers (described below) instead.

Privacy barriers that separate the front from the rear of the car can attract attention, but are better than nothing. To block the front windshield, you can purchase an inexpensive, reflective mylar sun shade cover or blocker (usually shaped like an accordion when unfolded across the dashboard) from most auto parts stores. Reflectix (mylar bubble wrap) is the least expensive option, and you can cut it to fit each window. If the shiny, silver mylar attracts attention, you can spray paint the exterior facing gray to dull the shine, without decreasing its effectiveness. If all else fails, you can take a plastic tarp that most matches your exterior vehicle color, and cut out pieces to fit each individual window, and use either tape or velcro to hold them up. Velcro is preferable because it's quicker and easier to remove the window coverings when you need to drive, and replace them when you want privacy. Use curtains and rods only if they are practical for your vehicle (such as vans), and if you have the equipment and know-how to install them properly.

If your windows aren't tinted or covered, obscure your belongings neatly with a neutral-colored blanket, sheet or tarp, depending on the color of your car interior. In other words, do not use a bright blue tarp to cover your belongings if your interior is light gray and your car color is black. A white- or cream-colored sheet would be far more appropriate, and can easily be acquired from thrift stores. Store bedding in the trunk when not in use, instead of the back seat. If you have to use the back seat or back floor for storage, be sure to cover items using the above guidelines.

What to Keep Near

You'll want to keep the following items within arm's reach at all times:[19]

- Car keys
- Blankets and pillows
- Towels and wash cloths
- Full water jugs or bottles
- Food
- Toilet receptacle
- Cell phone and charger for emergencies
- Money for gas
- Car insurance proof and drivers license

Car insurance is mandatory in almost all states, and the most vital document you must carry with you in the vehicle. You can drop your rates by insuring just the minimum amount required by law for your state.[20] If you have been homeless for a while, you may not have money for car insurance. If you can't afford it, ask a friend or family member to pay your premium for you until you can get back on your feet again and repay them. This is crucial, because if you are caught driving without insurance, in many states your vehicle will be ticketed and towed on the spot, and impounded. And you won't be able to recover the vehicle until you pay the ticket, the impound fees, and provide proof of insurance—a triple whammy of heavy expenses! If you're living in your car and this happens, it's pretty much game over and you are out on the streets.

Other items to keep close at hand are:

- Scissors to open food packaging and trim out window coverings
- Drinking water bottle
- Flashlight, to use at night to fumble around the car looking for things
- Gym membership (a place to stay clean and work off stress)

Clothes should be stored inside black trash bags used as a liner inside small suitcases. A soft-sided suitcase is best, but failing that, just double-bagging your clothes in the black trash bags serves two purposes: 1) It prevents condensation from smelling up your clothes with mildew, and 2) They are soft and flexible if you have to lean against them while sleeping. Store non-seasonal clothing in a storage unit.

If you are going to stay in one location for awhile, buy a bus pass or ticket book as a back-up for emergencies, such as vehicle repairs.

Living Space and Vehicle Type

Utilize your car space effectively. Draw a picture of your car's interior and trunk and try to figure out where you will place things. In my stationwagon I had 75 cubic feet of space for my bedding, boxes of food, clothing, laundry items, hardware, cat food, and my cat's food and water dishes. (75 cubic feet is equal to approximately 17.78 square feet.) By comparison, a standard-sized casket is 84 x 28 x 23, which is roughly 31.3 cubic feet, or 9.93 square feet.[21] So the space I lived in is roughly the size of two caskets.

If you are in a sedan, a general rule of thumb is that food and water go on the front floor and passenger seat, covered by a bath towel (or folded sheet) matching your car interior so as not to attract attention and to protect against sunlight. The back seat area of the car is for sleeping. If you don't have a late model sedan with front seats that fold forward to make a flat surface, you can stack bags of clothing on the rear floor to help support your legs and give you a wider sleeping area in the back seat. Tuck in seat belt buckles under the cushions. Extra blankets or bath towels can be used to level the car seats into a flatter surface. You can cover your pillow and a suitcase (or plastic bag) of clothes with your blankets while storing them on the back seat (neatly folded) during the day. Items that you don't use on a daily basis can go in the trunk, such as more suitcases of clothing, extra toiletries, documents, etc.

If you are in a station wagon or SUV, food and water will go in the front passenger floor and seat area, covered. Obviously the back seats will be folded down to maximize sleeping room. In some SUV's, you'll have to lay in the back diagonally to fully stretch out. Otherwise, it's best to line one side of the back sleeping area with boxes and suitcases, and have your bedding laid out on the other side. (You may need to secure your stacked boxes and suitcases with a few bungee cords, or clothesline, to keep them from toppling over while you drive.) The advantage of an SUV or stationwagon is that you don't have to put your bedding away each day; you can just cover it up or leave it as is if people can't see in.

If you are in a minivan or box van, you have a lot of room; almost a mini-apartment on wheels. Minivans often have the ability to fold the back seats directly into the floor (in older models, they have to be removed entirely and placed in storage), and allow for 150 cubic feet (almost 30 square feet) of cargo space. That's big enough for a bathroom space, sleeping area, and a large amount of storage, with food and water kept up front for easy access. The downside of both minivans and box vans is horrible gas mileage. But if you're going to stay in one area for a long time, they are excellent.

If you are traveling with a pet, a cat litterbox fits well on the passenger side floor. Or, if you're bringing other small animals, you can place cages or pet beds there instead. [See: Pets]

4. DURING CAR LIVING: SITUATIONS & SCENARIOS

The first week is the hardest as you adjust your plans to reality: putting items into and removing things from storage, purchasing necessities you forgot, or which arose as a sudden need. Expect to be stressed and uncomfortable at first. It's a huge adjustment to make, going from a house to essentially one step away from living on the streets. It can take a few days for the shock to wear off.

Car living habits in a large city with a warm climate (such as Phoenix, Arizona) can vary significantly from what you'd do in a small city with a cool climate, such as Olympia, Washington. Conversely, what plays in Seattle won't necessarily work in El Centro, California. You will have to discern for yourself the difference between what's uncomfortable (i.e., a cold vehicle in the winter) and what's intolerable (living in the car during a three-day blizzard, or hundred-plus degree heat wave).

Understand up front that most elements of car living are inherently mildly to moderately uncomfortable. When things start consistently crossing the line into severely uncomfortable, and into the realm of intolerable, you will have to come up with a plan to get out of the situation somehow, even if only temporarily. There is a huge difference between discomfort and abject misery. Usually the latter can be prevented with some foresight and ingenuity. And as always, money helps.

Based on your location, think ahead and plan for emergencies. For example, what will you do in a snowstorm? Where will you park to keep the car from being buried? Where will you eat? Is it possible for you to stash emergency cash for motels in such a situation?

You will also have to choose whether to stay centrally located or be mobile. Staying centrally located is easier if you have a set place to stay. A best-case scenario is if you have a friend or relative with property near town where you can park long-term, even if you pay $100 a month or so for rent if you're working or collecting unemployment. It also helps if you live in a town or city large enough to have public transportation. That way, you are walking everywhere (or using public transit) and just using the vehicle to sleep in. Make sure you don't park in metered or timed zones if you are centrally located. You don't want something to happen where you may be gone from the vehicle for longer than you had planned, and by the time you return, your vehicle will have been ticketed and towed. The majority of car dwellers, however, tend to be mobile, taking the car with them to work and elsewhere, with no permanent or long-term place to park.

Bathrooms, Showers, & Toilets

Restrooms are incredibly easy to find; take your pick:

- Libraries
- Public buildings (i.e., city hall, court house)
- Gas stations
- Convenience stores
- Fast food restaurants
- Grocery stores
- Cafes
- Rest stops
- Truck stops
- Community centers
- City or state welcome centers or tourist bureaus

If you can't find any of those locations, or there aren't any nearby, look for a construction site (either housing or commercial) since they usually have Porta Potties.

There are two types of bathrooms: fully enclosed and multi-stalled. A fully-enclosed bathroom is a room that only one person can be in at a time, and it has a sink and toilet. These are a car dweller's best friend, and can be found at major coffee chains or most gas stations. A multi-stalled public restroom is what you'll find at most libraries, big box discount stores, or fast-food places, where there are several sinks and toilet stalls all in one big room.

Wherever you decide to go to change clothes, clean up, and use the toilet, using the fabric-like, recycled, grocery tote bags to carry your soap, washcloths, towels and change of clothes won't attract attention to your intent, especially if you are using a grocery store restroom. Bring trial-size bottles, as they are easily concealed in your sack or tote bag while you are in stores and bathrooms. Refill them from larger bottles kept in your car or storage unit.

You can brush your teeth easily without a bathroom, as a small cup of water can double as a sink. You can use it to rinse your mouth and toothbrush, and then dump the cup of water away from the car on nearby landscaping. (Men can also shave using a similar method.)

SHOWERS

Showering is the most pressing need when living out of your car. If you smell bad, it will be a dead giveaway that you are homeless, and the prejudice against you will rise dramatically. As one former car dweller put it:

> "Always bathe. If you look like a homeless person, then people will treat you like dirt. When I was homeless, I bathed at the L.A. Free Clinic, the West Hollywood Pool, and I took a lot of sponge baths at places where I could lock the bathroom door...I am also told that many community colleges have showers and locker facilities where people can bathe."[22]

You basically have several choices here, depending on your location (city, rural town, etc.). The most expensive options are either a gym, health club or YMCA membership. These memberships are especially good if you are going to be mobile, because you can go anywhere in the country where that particular club or franchise has a location and use the facility. You can also rent a locker to store interview clothes.

Public pools offer shower facilities, and you can usually either pay a per-visit fee, or buy a monthly pass or multi-visit discount punch card for far less than the cost of most gym memberships. However, many public pools only operate during the summer months. If so, check out community colleges with athletic facilities. They often have community education classes you can enroll in for far less than the cost of a gym or YMCA membership over the span of a few months. For example, a power volleyball class that meets once a week costs $25 for three months. But the enrollment credential allows you to use the gym facilities every day during that time span.

Less expensive options include state parks, but you have to check which ones are open year round, have shower facilities, and if there is a day use fee (anywhere from $5-$10) on top of the cheap shower fee (it varies, but usually $1.00 for five minutes of hot water using park tokens). Some state parks waive the day use fee if you only use the restroom and shower facilities. Many public marinas have free restrooms and coin-operated shower facilities for a dollar or two, and sometimes you can get away with parking your car at the marina to sleep.

Some community centers have free showers. During the summer, some beaches do as well. If you can't find a shower location on the Internet, ask a local resident, or a librarian. Asking "Do you have a local recreation center with a swimming pool and shower facilities?" won't tip off that you are homeless. Truck stops with showers can easily be found via a basic Internet search, but can be costly: $6 or more, unless you can score a shower credit from a sympathetic truck driver.

You don't *have* to take a bath or shower to stay clean; you can take a sponge bath, which involves washing your whole body with wet washcloths (or a sponge, hence the name) rather than taking a bath or shower. You can do this in the car if you have privacy, or a restroom if not, to stay clean between showers. To spongebathe, you'll need three washcloths, soap, and a sink, or a full bottle of warm water if doing so in the car. Use one wet washcloth with soap to clean, one wet and soap-free washcloth to rinse, and one to dry.

If possible, invest in an agave cloth rather than a cotton wash cloth when showering and taking sponge baths. The agave mesh will dry quicker, and your skin will stay cleaner longer, because agave cloths slough off dead skin cells. You can find them in natural food stores or co-ops. They are expensive ($6-$10), but they last a long time.

The hardest part of staying clean while car living is washing your hair (and for women, styling it). The best way is to find an enclosed restroom, preferably located on the exterior of a building, like those found at gas stations and convenience stores, rather than a multi-stalled restroom like public libraries, where patrons will see you with your head in the sink and report you. If you do wash your hair in the sink at convenience stores or elsewhere, be sure to clean the hair out of the sink before you leave, *and* use the air hand dryer to dry your hair so you don't walk out into the lobby with a wet head. Both will get you banned from using the location again, and are just plain rude anyway.

If you can't find a suitable restroom, use a large, plastic water bottle filled with warm water to wet, shampoo and rinse your hair outside of your car. (This is not fun during cold weather.) If you don't have access to warm water, you can wrap the bottle in dark plastic (such as standard lawn and leaf bags), fill it, and leave it on your dashboard to warm up during the day —if it's sunny. You can also buy solar shower kits online, or even make your own out of a plastic soda bottle, if you have access to an abundant water supply. You can then use towels, the car door, and the cover of darkness for privacy.

Good: Spongebath. Better: College campus gym, truck stop, public pool or beach with showers. Best: YMCA, fitness club or private gym membership, if you have the money.

TOILETS

What do you do when you have to go in the middle of the night, and there's no fast food restaurant or convenience store around, and you can't risk being detected? For men, a plastic bottle with a cap is simple and easy enough. Women have to work a little harder; a plastic dairy container with cat litter inside is a lifesaver!

To make a toilet container, you will need:

- A large, plastic, lidded butter or margarine tub, which come in 2 or 3 lb. sizes. (You can also use large, plastic food storage containers with lids. Try to get the large bowl sizes that hold 7 cups/56 ounces.)
- Two large plastic freezer zip bags (preferably gallon size)
- A roll of toilet paper
- Some cat litter (preferably pine, not clay). You don't *have* to use cat litter if you can't afford the expense, but one 7 lb. bag of pine cat litter costs less than $4.00, and will last a long time (2-3 months or longer, since you don't use much). It will also neutralize odor and prevent a nasty mess in your car if you accidentally tip and spill the container. It is also easier to dispose of than clay litter.

Place a couple of handfuls of cat litter in one of the plastic zip bags. Enclose that plastic zip bag within the second plastic zip bag. Place both in the plastic tub, and fold the bag openings around the top edge of the tub to hold them open. Position the tub underneath you, and do what you need to do. Then, seal each individual zip bag within the butter tub, and seal the lid on the tub. If you use a large amount of cat litter, this method will be good for several uses before you'll have to dispose of it. Using pine cat litter is best, as it is entirely biodegradable, and can be disposed of as mulch around the base of shrubs if you aren't near a trash can.

If you have a bigger vehicle, or don't feel comfortable with the plastic tub positioning, you can also use a five-gallon bucket with a lid for toilet needs. Many grocery store bakeries, and construction sites, have standard, five-gallon buckets with lids you can clean and re-use, and they are often free for the asking.[23] If you use clay cat litter, it usually comes in smaller, two- or three-gallon buckets with a lid, which may be more suitable for smaller vehicles. If you have money, and want to buy something designed rather than improvised, check out the Luggable Loo or other bucket toilets with seat-like, snap-on lids.

Keep a container of moist towelettes on hand (which you can get from a dollar store) to wipe and clean up with, particularly at night. Don't use hand sanitizers, as they will dry out your skin unnecessarily, since they contain isopropyl alcohol.

For solid human waste, it's far easier to simply find a restroom; however, that isn't always possible. In that case, keep some disposable, biodegradable plastic bags on hand to use. (These can usually be found in natural food stores—they are used to line kitchen compost bins in major cities.) Biodegradable plastic bags are made of cornstarch, and tend to be expensive ($6-$8 for a roll of 10), but are worth it if you have to bury human waste. It is illegal to dump human solid waste in trash containers, so dumping the bag contents in a toilet next time you are around one, or burying the entire bag underground in rural areas, will keep conditions sanitary for everyone.[24] To bury it properly, dig a hole a minimum of six inches deep (you can use a sharp rock to dig if you don't keep a shovel in the trunk of your car), deposit the bag, and then cover up the hole with dirt.[25]

Children

Forty one percent of the homeless population is made up of families with children, the fastest growing group of homeless people in the country.[26] Most of them (85%) are headed by single women with children.[27] Forty-two percent of children in homeless families are under age six.[28] Approximately 21 percent of homeless families live in places not intended for housing, such as cars, public spaces, etc.[29]

Since I don't have children, or first-hand experience car living with children, I can only offer a few important basics here to point you in the right direction:

1) Kids who lack a fixed and adequate nighttime residence have difficulties with school enrollment, attendance and success.[30] If you are car living in or near the same city where your kids attend school, they can continue to attend their original school. The school district provides appropriate transportation (which can be a taxi, a public bus system, etc.) to and from the classroom in these cases.

During homelessness, kids need to maintain a "normal" routine during the day, similar to adults who live in cars at night but work during the day. It keeps them out of the vehicle, and takes their mind off their predicament, while providing a shred of stability. Schools offer many important benefits, including safety, predictability, a sense of normalcy, adult and peer support, meals, basic medical and mental health services, and extracurricular activities. Schools can also connect families to other resources and supports available in the community.[31]

The McKinney-Vento Act is a federal law that ensures children and youth who have lost their housing can attend school. It covers children and youth who are living in domestic violence shelters, emergency shelters, transitional living programs, staying temporarily with friends or relatives due to the lack of adequate accommodations, and staying in motels, campgrounds, *cars*, or other temporary or inadequate housing.[32]

The McKinney-Vento Act says that children who have lost their housing can:

- Attend school, no matter where they live, or how long they have lived there.
- Continue in the school they went to before losing their housing, or in the school in which they were enrolled last (called "school of origin"), even if they move out of the school district, if that is feasible.
- Go to the local school in the area where they are living. The school must immediately let students enroll, attend classes, and participate fully in school activities, even if students do not have a parent or guardian with them, or documents such as proof of residency, immunization records, other medical records, or school records.
- Receive transportation to their school of origin, provided or arranged by the school district.
- Access all the school services they need, including preschool.
- Go to school with children who are not in temporary housing and be free from harassment. Students cannot be separated from the regular school program because of their housing.
- Have disagreements with the school settled quickly, and go to the school they choose while disagreements are settled.
- Contact the school district homeless education liaison, whose job is to help children in homeless situations enroll and succeed in school.[33]

Every state is required by federal law to have a state coordinator for homeless education. This person is responsible for ensuring the understanding of and compliance with the McKinney-Vento Act in public schools throughout the state. To find the contact for your state, call the National Center for Homeless Education toll-free helpline at 1-800-308-2145, visit http://center.serve.org/nche/states/state_resources.php#map, or email homeless@serve.org.

2) Far more public services and housing programs are available to families with children than single homeless people. One crucial lifeline is Temporary Assistance for Needy Families (TANF), a federal program that provides cash assistance and supportive services to families with children under age 18.[34] To find out how to apply for TANF in your state, call 2-1-1, or visit http://www.acf.hhs.gov/programs/ofa/help and select your state from the list.

One of the biggest problems with children living in vehicles is the parents' fear that if they apply for public assistance, the children will be taken from them and placed into custody of Child Protective Services (CPS) or a foster home, because they are living in a car. Their fears are not unfounded:

- Homeless children are at particularly high risk for being placed in foster care: 12% of homeless children have been placed in foster care, compared to 1% of other children.

- Families who have experienced homelessness have much higher rates of family separation than other low-income families. Homelessness is also a barrier to reunification for some families. At least 30% of children in foster care could return home if their parents had access to housing.[35]

To find out what your rights are in your area, call your local Human Services office anonymously, or check Appendix A in the back of this book to find free legal assistance in your area, so you can apply for benefits without fear.

The Child Support Enforcement programs in each state can be a helpful resource to families consisting of single custodial parents with children, since one of the reasons for the homelessness may be non-payment of child support. In addition, child support programs can help homeless noncustodial parents address any outstanding child support issues (i.e., helping them with the order modification process). These programs can also connect them with organizations that can help with basic skills, such as how to seek and maintain employment, and understand issues surrounding court and child support agency processes.[36]

3) This is the hardest part: You have to get kids to understand that it's not safe to tell people they are living in a car. They have to lie, and tell people they are staying with friends. This isn't so hard to do with teenagers, but younger children especially make terrible liars. Unfortunately, since the majority of their parents' time is engrossed in day-to-day survival, car dwelling children learn to stay in the background, out of the way, and practically invisible, at a time in their lives when receiving attention and having their emotional needs met should be at the forefront.

Homeless children often respond to their situation in one of two ways: 1) They either dive into their schoolwork with deep fervor, as it provides an escape from thinking about their circumstances, or 2) They know something bad is going on, and may act out, either in class or in public.

As with adults, being without a home takes a terrible physical and mental toll on children.[37] For example:

- Homeless children are sick at twice the rate of other children. They suffer twice as many ear infections, have four times the rate of asthma, and have five times more diarrhea and stomach problems.
- Homeless children go hungry twice as often as non-homeless children.
- More than one-fifth of homeless preschoolers have emotional problems serious enough to require professional care, but less than one-third receive any treatment.
- Homeless children are twice as likely to repeat a grade compared to non-homeless children.

- Homeless children have twice the rate of learning disabilities, and three times the rate of emotional and behavioral problems of non-homeless children.
- Half of school-age homeless children experience anxiety, depression, or withdrawal, compared to 18 percent of non-homeless children.
- By the time homeless children are eight years old, one in three has a major mental disorder.[38]

Homelessness often leads to frequent moving and upheaval, which eliminates feelings of safety, stability, and predictability that are so important for healthy growth. Homelessness forces kids to grow up fast in a very stressful environment. If it's possible (and safe) for relatives or friends to take your children in temporarily, they can avoid adding to the statistics.

Climates: Hot & Cold

Keep in mind that the outdoor temperature in both hot and cold weather will be the minimum indoor temperature of your vehicle. Cars are not insulated like houses, because car manufacturers do not anticipate that you will be living in them. Even if you attempt to insulate your vehicle, you won't be able to substantially mitigate the greenhouse effects of the sun on glass, or the winter chill of the car body metal, to any degree that will make it worth the time or expense.   You will still need fans, spray misters and ice packs in the summer, and heaters, multiple clothing layers, and several heavy blankets in the winter.

Don't leave the car running for heat or air conditioning, because you will need to conserve gas. If you work in a climate-controlled store or office during the day, consider yourself lucky. To avoid temperature extremes during the day if you are unemployed, there are a number of places you can go to protect yourself from the weather:

- Library
- Cafes, restaurants, and coffee shops

- Large chain book stores
- Gym or fitness center
- Large grocery stores, or big box stores with snack bars
- Parks and hiking trails
- Free art galleries or museums
- Shopping malls
- Bars or casinos

In the winter, taking a hot shower, or soaking in a hot tub at the gym in the morning will erase your overnight chill. In the summer, swimming or showering at night will keep you clean and cool, and make it easier to fall asleep.

Summer Car Living

Warm weather presents the opposite problem of cold, because if it's cold, you can always pile on more and more layers of clothing and additional blankets. When it's warm, however, you can only go down to bare skin. Particularly problematic are desert Southwest areas such as Arizona, where the heat lingers in triple figures late into the night and very early morning, and the humid climates of the Southeast. If you can leave a desert-based climate for a cooler one during the heat of the summer, do so. Otherwise, look for cooler altitudes near you and consider staying there. For example, Phoenix, Arizona gets ridiculously hot during the summer, but Flagstaff, two hours away, is tolerable. Conversely, in winter, if you can, seek out a warmer climate.

In hot climates, finding a swimming pool or a gym with showers you can use regularly is imperative. Ice water, a spray bottle, and washcloths will help cool you via skin surface evaporation. You can get a small scoop of ice for free from a convenience store if you ask first. Buy a spray bottle at a dollar store, fill it up with ice cold water (mix ice 50/50 with water) and spray or mist your skin frequently. When you go to bed, wet a washcloth, towel, or shirt with ice water, and place it on your skin. You can also put ice in a hot water bladder or doubled, zip plastic bags, and place it on top of your pillow to stay cool, instead of using wet rags. Keep a sheet beneath you, particularly in sedans, to keep sweat from staining both leather and cloth seats.

Purchase inexpensive, reflective sun shades from an auto parts store for both the front and back windows. During the day, ruthlessly look for shaded areas to park your car, and move the vehicle to follow the shade as the sun transits. Public parking garages can be immensely helpful if your area has them, and they don't cost a fortune to park in. You can also purchase inexpensive, solar- or battery-powered fans, or 12-volt fans that work from your car's cigarette lighter. Solar fans won't work at night or when it's cloudy, and battery-powered fans can get expensive because of having to replace the batteries from constant use.

In hot weather, you can find public pools, ponds, streams, rivers or lakes to swim in to cool off. Some cities have public water parks that are designed for patrons to get splashed or sprayed.[39] You can try to surreptitiously slip into a hotel or apartment complex pool as well. Shower or swim often, especially in the evening so you can go to sleep cool and clean. Expect local swimming pools, rivers, parks and beaches to be crowded during summer. Many parks have a day use fee, but you can purchase an annual pass which can easily pay for itself the first month. The annual parks pass will also give you unlimited access to restrooms, a place to cook, and a place to swim or shower for less than the cost of a gym membership. In some areas, it's safe to sleep on the car roof, or in a sleeping bag near the vehicle. (Place the sleeping bag on a large, plastic trash bag sliced open lengthwise to keep ground moisture and dirt away.)

Higher elevations (>2,000 feet) cool down at night much quicker than valleys and desert basins, which act as heat sinks. Also, avoid asphalt and concrete (downtown areas) in favor of grassy areas with shade trees (suburbs). Being near a body of water can also decrease temperatures, but keep in mind that without a decent breeze, you'll have mosquito to contend with.

No one wants to suffocate from stifling heat or humidity, but open windows in the evening are a security risk. If you feel the risk is small for your particular location, you can buy inexpensive screen mesh at any hardware store, cut it to fit your window size, secure it in place with velcro, and roll it up and store it in the trunk when not in use. A more expensive option ($200-$250) in a hot climate is to buy window vents from auto accessory shops. The vents will permit air flow, and prevent condensation from forming, while your car windows remain closed.[40] A body shop can paint the vents to match your car color and mount them for you.

Winter Car Living

Trying to heat an uninsulated vehicle consistently is a lost cause. It is far easier (and less expensive) to warm your body, and then keep it that way by insulating yourself with several layers of clothes and blankets, than trying to retrofit your car to resemble a stryofoam box. If you are cold, you will have enormous difficulty sleeping, period. This is your body's way of trying to protect you. Even in summer, late night fog or a storm can bring an unexpected chill to a car that is downright uncomfortable.

Luckily, in the winter, many cities and churches open up temporary shelters on nights when the weather drops below 32 degrees. These shelters are far better from a safety standpoint than regular, permanent shelters. Some temporary shelters even allow pets. However, if there are no shelters in your area, and winter car living is unavoidable, you'll need the following items to keep you from being utterly miserable:

- A sleeping bag (down is best) good to $0°$ degrees or lower. You can sleep on top of it for cushioning in the summer, and inside it in the winter. Shop around online, at thrift stores, recycled or discount sporting goods stores, or at big box discount retailers. Some larger cities have organizations that acquire and donate free sleeping bags to homeless people.[41]
- A heavy down comforter, or wool blankets. Down comforters and wool blankets are excellent to sleep on

top of to prevent chassis chill, and to lay under to keep warm. They are bulky, but worth it, and essential if you don't have a heater.

- A down jacket. Buy one used in a thrift store, or new in discount or outlet stores, for roughly $30 or less. You can buy premium down in the off-season at steep discounts from catalog retailers who specialize in outdoor goods.

- Ski pants or sweatpants from thrift stores, or new at discount or outlet stores. Try to buy a size or two larger than you normally wear, since you will slip them on over your jeans and other layers at night before you sleep.

- Windshield de-icer by the gallon (Prestone Yellow is best). It's cheaper than smaller spray cans and much more effective, particularly in wind chill. It is especially helpful during times of freezing fog. If your windshield washer fluid sprayer doesn't work, you can put it in any empty spray bottle and store the remainder of the gallon in your storage unit. It's a lifesaver when it comes to defrosting your windows quickly.

- A 12-volt, fleece, electric blanket for roughly $25. The blanket plugs into your car cigarette lighter, and has an auto-shutoff feature so it won't drain your battery overnight.[42]

- An extremely helpful item to have on hand (literally) are disposable hand warmers that can be purchased by the box at discount retailers, sporting goods stores, and occasionally at dollar stores. They are small individual packets that produce heat by activating powdered, non-toxic chemicals when rubbed. You can also buy reusable hand warmers, but they need to be submerged in water to regenerate.

Before you go to bed, if you have a gym membership, go and take a hot shower, or soak in the hot tub. This will warm you up considerably, which will give all the layers and gear you have to wear to keep warm in the car a head start in insulating you. Sleep in multiple layers of clothing, and under several layers of blankets. Wear wool socks and a hat to bed. Down booties (or any type of slippers) over the wool socks will keep your feet warm most of the night. I used to sleep in a long-sleeved, silk blouse under a fleece shirt, fleece pants, and wore a scarf, gloves, fleece jacket and down vest, and two pairs of wool socks and fleece slippers. All of that *and* underneath a heavy down comforter, with two fleece blankets on top of it. At 27 degrees, I still ended up cold by morning, anyway.

Some car dwellers recommend sleeping with a warm water bottle, but you first have to have a place to obtain the warm water (such as the gym, before you leave for the evening to sleep in the car), and you have to have enough room in your bedding to use it comfortably. If you don't have a flexible, bladder-type water bottle, then a few small, 8-oz. plastic water bottles may do the trick.

The most effective (but slightly expensive) way to stay warm is via catalytic heaters.[43] Catalytic heaters don't require electricity, are extremely safe, and while still needing proper ventilation due to the amount of oxygen they remove from the immediate area (hypoxia), they produce very little carbon monoxide. (If you want to be on the safe side, you can purchase a battery-powered carbon monoxide detector for around $25.) But some catalytic heater models include a low-oxygen shut-off switch for safe indoor operation. Be sure to allow for adequate ventilation to compensate for the oxygen being used by the heater. And be careful enough to locate the heater in a safe place in the vehicle so you don't melt or set fire to your upholstery or blankets. Use common sense.

There are two particular catalytic heater lines that are well-suited for car living, because they are intended for RVs. One is the Mr. Heater company's Buddy line, which is best for most moderate winter climates (e.g., where temperatures rarely go to zero, such as the Pacific Northwest). Mr. Heater brand makes a model called Little Buddy (3,800 BTU) that is designed to heat rooms of up to 100 square feet, which is more than enough for your car.

The other brand of catalytic heater well-suited for car living is the Olympian company's Wave line for the harshest winter climates (such as Alaska and the Midwest). Olympian makes the Wave 3 and the Wave 6 models (the Wave 8 is too hot for small spaces like cars, and will melt your vehicle interior, if not set it on fire outright). The Wave 3 model, which outputs 3000 BTU, costs slightly less than $200, while the Wave 6 (6000 BTU) costs around $250 (neither include propane, refill adapters, or hose assemblies, which cost extra). So for $50 more, you get double the output of the Wave 3.

The Mr. Buddy heaters will burn more propane than the Olympian Wave heaters, as the Olympian heaters use low pressure for the liquid propane (LP) rather than high. Also, some users have reported the Buddy heaters won't run in high altitudes (5,000 feet and above), but the Olympian is rated for altitudes of up to 12,000 feet. Choose the one that best suits your region and budget.

As far as fuel costs, a single 16 oz. propane cylinder (approximately $40) can provide heat for up to 14 hours at 1,500 BTU. It should last a little while, because you are only running it long enough to take the chill out of the car, and small spaces heat up quickly. So if you run it for ten minutes in the morning, and ten in the evening, for a total of 20 minutes per day at 3,000 BTU, a 14-hour canister should last 21 days.

What you don't want is for all that heat to be lost by cold coming through all of the windows. You can use Reflectix, which is basically insulating mylar bubble wrap, and cut it to the size of your windows and press it (or velcro it, or duct tape it) into place to prevent heat loss, especially from the windshield. A roll of Reflectix that is 16 inches x 25 feet is more than enough for most vehicles, and costs less than $20. You can buy it at most hardware stores.

So basically, for $20 for Reflectix as window covering, a Little Buddy heater for $75, plus propane, hoses and adapters for approximately $50, staying warm in intolerably cold temperatures costs less than $150. It's an excellent investment (and far cheaper than a motel or hostel) if you have the money to purchase the heaters and peripherals before car living. Not being able to afford to do so was my single biggest mistake (and regret) in my car living experience.

After settling on a heat source, and using Reflectix as window insulation at night, the next ounce of prevention is to use a divider to separate the front of the car from the back where you sleep. A divider reduces the size of the area you need to heat, provides privacy, and helps prevent condensation on the windows. To create a divider, string a piece of clothesline across the ceiling and tie the ends to the handles on the ceiling above the doors. Then, hang a mylar blanket or super-size piece of Reflectix on the side where you sleep, and a blanket (or sheet) facing the driving area. Clothespins or large safety pins will secure the two pieces to the clothesline.

You can also take a king-sized bath towel and drape it across the front seat headrests to block most of the center gap between the front seats. Try to use a dark color so you don't have a glaring white sheet looking out of place at night, and attracting attention. This method will mainly prevent visibility more than block the cold, due to the gap between the ceiling and headrests.

During the day, point the windshield in the direction of the sun, so it heats the interior of the vehicle (this is known as passive solar gain). If you park your car facing east at night, and there's frost, the sun will melt the ice on the windshield for you in the morning, saving you from having to get out and scrape, or spray de-icer.

You can avoid the cold during the day by spending your time in the same places listed previously above for hot weather. If you're unemployed, in the winter shopping malls provide a warm environment with bathrooms (and expensive food). The larger the city, the more malls you can rotate between each day to stay inconspicuous, if you have the gas money to do so. Malls are open late hours in winter to accommodate holiday shopping, so you can stay warm indoors longer. So you can spend the morning in a coffee shop, the afternoon at the library, and then head to the mall when the library closes, until it's time to go back to the car to sleep. Or you can spend the day at one mall, and switch to another in the evening.

And sometimes, in some places (e.g., beach, rural setting), it's just a good idea to build a good, old-fashioned bonfire.

In the event of a winter storm watch, you don't want to be immobilized for days by having your vehicle buried under snow and ice. What to do?

Try to find a covered parking garage at colleges, malls, office buildings, hotels, etc.), or an apartment complex, or any other location with a protective overhang. If you are questioned, explain that you are from out of town (especially plausible if you have license plates from a different state) and you pulled over to ride out the storm safely. Do not say you are living out of your vehicle. The storm is the perfect cover to keep the inquisitor from calling the cops or a tow truck, because they know you'll be on your way once the storm passes.

Good: 12-volt cigarette lighter plug-in blankets. Better: Little Buddy or Olympian Wave 3 catalytic heater. Best: Spending time at the indoor locations listed above.

Communications: Cell Phones, Computers, Internet/WiFi, & Mail

The Internet and cell phones have made staying connected while homeless easier to do. If you cannot afford any kind of cellphone whatsoever, there's a government program called Safelink that provides individuals who qualify with a free cell phone, and up to 250 minutes a month. (If you already participate in food stamps/SNAP, Medicaid, or other social services program, you are probably eligible.[44]) Contact Safelink at 1-800-SafeLink (1-800-723-3546), or visit their website at www.safelinkwireless.com to see what the eligibility requirements are for your state, and to enroll.

If you don't qualify for Safelink, or you live outside the U.S., prepaid cell phones are a bargain. For roughly $20, you can get a basic cellphone with double or triple minute plans, text and web access. Also, pay-as-you-go phones are far less expensive than a contracted phone, and often use the same networks (such as AT&T). Keep in mind, though, that pay-as-you-go phones are best for emergencies and setting up job interview appointments. They are not cost-effective for long family chats.

If you're not employed, and therefore can't recharge your cell phone at work, you can recharge it at your gym (if you have a membership), or in a library or cafe—just make sure it's kept in sight at all times. Put a sticker (such as a blank address label) on the back of the phone with your email address on it, so that if you lose or forget it, you can be contacted and it can be returned to you.

If you don't want to go the cellphone route at all, you can still make and receive calls and voicemails, and send and receive texts, if you have computer access. Sign up for Google Voice, which provides unlimited free calls and text messages to anywhere in the U.S. and Canada. (At the time of this writing, Google Voice is only available for sign-up if you live U.S.). The service is free, and it can send you an email notification each time you receive a voicemail. You can retrieve your voicemail from any phone or computer anywhere (such as a landline). You can also listen to the message via computer speakers when you are online. Messages can also be transcribed in case you don't have access to audio on the computer.

The other great thing about Google Voice is that your phone number can be a permanent number regardless of where you live in the U.S. So if you move clear across the country, people can still call the original number, and you can have the calls forwarded to your new local cell or landline phone without missing a call.

COMPUTERS

Ask yourself this: Can you afford to have your computer stolen? Because computers, cell phones and money are exactly what vehicle prowlers are looking for when selecting their next victim. If the answer is no, have a friend or relative hold your computer for safekeeping, or put it in your storage unit. Before you do, back up your computer files to a USB drive that you keep with you, and you will essentially have your computer readily at hand. (At the time of this writing, an 8GB USB drive on sale at big box office supply stores costs less than $10.) You can also back up and store your data with free, online, cloud storage services, such as Google Drive. If you have to have a computer, alternatives are to buy a less expensive netbook or touchscreen pad (each are roughly $99), or use a smartphone with Web access if you can afford the contract.

Libraries and most coffee shops have free wireless Internet. If you don't have a wireless device, most libraries will allow non-residents 15 minutes of computer and Internet time if you ask for a guest pass. Note of caution: Be careful of the location of the library branch you visit. Some have security warnings posted about being in high-theft or car prowl areas. Heed the warnings and use computers at a safer location, such as another branch, or a cafe. These venues also provide protection from the weather (and time out of your car), as well as restroom access. Many motel chains have free wireless as well, but the networks may be password protected. If you drive around with your netbook on, you can often find an open, unsecured connection in a shopping center or residential area. In rural areas, this may be more difficult, and prepaid mobile broadband via a wireless USB modem may be the only (and expensive) option.

Good: Smartphone with Internet access. Better: Using a netbook or touchpad at a major coffee chain, or other commercial establishment advertising free WiFi. You can also usually access the signal from the parking lot. Best: Libraries and cafes.

MAIL

You can rent a U.S. Postal Service P.O. Box either in person or online.[45] From their website (http://www.usps.com), you can choose a location and box size, fill out the application online, and print it to take to the post office where you're renting the box. Whether you apply online or at a post office, to get a PO Box number and pick up your keys, you'll need to show two valid IDs: One must contain a photograph, and the other must prove your physical address.[46] Both must be current.

Acceptable forms of ID include:

- Valid driver's license or state ID card.
- Military, government, university, or recognized corporate ID.
- Passport, alien registration card, or certificate of naturalization.
- Current lease, mortgage, or deed of trust.
- Voter or vehicle registration card.
- Home or vehicle insurance policy.[47]

Be aware that your birth certificate, Social Security card, and credit cards are *not* valid forms of ID.[48]

Since you have to show a physical address, and not necessarily proof of residency, it's easiest if you rent the P.O. Box before living in your car. If not, don't worry—you can simply use your old address by showing the required documents with your old address on them. The post office requires that your box application (PS Form 1093) must always be current, and that as soon as any information changes (such as your street address, telephone number, or email address), you must update the information.[49] However, the worst that can happen for failing to do so is the post office may terminate your service.[50] This is highly unlikely, as being homeless means you have no address, and not that you are deliberately committing fraud. Talk with the postmaster directly, should any issue arise.

Prices vary for a U.S. Postal Service P.O. Box depending on the size of the city, and demand. In many moderate-sized towns, the cost is about $40 for six months, or $80 for a year. If you are planning to stay in one location for awhile, you can place a temporary forwarding order good for up to a year, and have your P.O. Box mail sent to you wherever you are, while still maintaining your original post office box address. Even without a P.O. Box, you can still temporarily forward mail from your old address to a friend or relative's address, for up to one year.

Sometimes a private, local mailbox or shipping company will have private mail boxes (PMBs, as opposed to POBs) that rent for less than the U.S. Postal Service PO Boxes. Shop around and compare prices.

A more expensive alternative is to hire a private mail-forwarding service. Some offer to scan your mail so you can read it online, receive packages and faxes for you, as well as check depositing services. Mail forwarding services tend to charge a monthly fee, and there are additional costs if you go over your monthly service plan allotment. Use the search engine term "mailbox forwarding" to see what's available and compare prices.

If you can't afford a mailbox from any source, see if you can ask a friend, relative, or neighbor to receive your mail for you. Give them several large mailing envelopes (8 1/2 x 11), and a book of stamps, so they can easily forward your mail to you. Sometimes, depending on your employer, you can have mail sent to your work address.

If all else fails, you can fill out a form either in person or online to have the post office at your last address hold your mail (and any packages) for you. They will only hold it for 30 days, unless you ask for a special exception because of your circumstances. You can schedule the service up to 30 days in advance, or by 2 a.m. CST (Mon-Sat) on the start date. Note that *all mail* for that address will be held, rather than an individual's mail.[51] When your mail hold ends, your can go and pick up your mail from the post office by presenting a photo ID.

As a last resort, general delivery is another option if you don't have a permanent address.[52] Mail addressed to you via general delivery will be held at the area's main post office for 10 days, or, if it is a check, 30 days.[53] To pick it up, you'll have to present a photo ID. Mail sent to you via general delivery should be addressed: Your Name, General Delivery, City, State, ZIP Code. In medium to large cities with multiple ZIP Codes, you'll want to make sure senders use the ZIP code for the area's main post office. To find the main post office in an area, ask a mail carrier or postal clerk, or call 1-800-ASK-USPS (1-800-275-8777).

If you are employed, have your paycheck set up for direct deposit, and sign up for online banking and online bill paying where possible. This will save you a lot of time, gas money, late fees and hassle, especially if easy or frequent access to your mail may be difficult.

Cooking, Food & Water

Since you won't have a refrigerator, in hot climates (such as the Southeast and Southwest), it is best to buy and consume food the same day. Make sure what you buy will withstand the temperature inside your car. Otherwise, you'll probably need a cooler, but will have to keep up with the expense of ice if it's not readily available from work or the gym. As such, note that items such as carrots (less than $1 per bag), lettuce ($0.99), or fruit such as bananas (.19 cents each), are cheaper than a bag of ice ($1.29). It's also not cost-effective to waste gas driving around looking for free sources of ice (such as convenience stores or motels). Food can last for days unrefrigerated in winter, especially if boxed and protected from the sun.

COOKING & REFRIGERATION

Some car dwellers keep an extra car battery on hand for extra power for cooking, refrigeration, heat, light, entertainment, etc. But these things are more suited to larger vehicles like vans, rather than cars. Getting electricity and power from a car battery for cooking and refrigeration is not covered in this book, nor is it recommended, as dual battery and inverter systems require some special expertise to assemble, and keep from blowing up the batteries (and yourself) in the process of use. There are many 12-volt appliances under $25 that you can run with an AC inverter (do an Internet search for "12-volt appliances") to power devices of 100 watts or less. But you'll run the risk of either draining your battery, or blowing the fuse.[54] And most of the 12-volt stoves, grills, refrigerators, air conditioners and frying pans aren't very effective anyway.[55] So when you add up the expense of purchasing these items, and the equipment needed to safely power them, you could have saved for a deposit on an apartment. It's not worth it for that hamburger or skillet of scrambled eggs, when both can easily be procured inexpensively, elsewhere, almost 24 hours a day.

The bottom line is that you don't really need electricity in the car. All you basically need is lighting, which a decent flashlight easily and inexpensively provides. Everything else you need electricity for, such as charging a phone or netbook, can be done at other locations such as libraries and cafes, and costs nothing.

I absolutely do not recommend trying to cook food on your car's engine. I also highly recommend against cooking inside cars for the following reasons: Having a flammable cooking device within inches of a 15-20 gallon gasoline tank beneath you is a recipe for disaster. Also, cooking inside the car with the windows closed is a serious carbon monoxide hazard. And with the windows open, people walking by will smell food coming from the vehicle. Is that pork chop really worth a knock on the window from the police? Especially since there are so many other, safer, options available.

As an alternative, convenience stores, gas stations and some motels will be happy to let you pop something in a microwave for a few minutes if you ask permission first. Food banks also tend to have microwaves. If you hate microwaves and absolutely must cook, buy an inexpensive propane cook stove (usually between $25-$100 depending on whether you get a single or double burner; don't forget propane canisters, refills, and adapter hoses cost extra), and cook outside in a park that has barbeque grills, or at a picnic area or rest area. Few people will be there around dusk, or after work, to bother you while you cook. If the weather is cold or rainy, you can wait in your vehicle while your food cooks outside.

If you choose to use a cooler to store perishable food, you can freeze bottled water at work (dump some out first to allow for expansion) rather than use ice, so you don't end up with food floating in water. Keep the cooler covered with blankets and pillows to provide extra insulation. In hot climates, buying ice in the summer can be a necessary evil, rather than wasting gas to go to a grocery store to buy food for immediate or same day consumption.

Sometimes it's a hassle to find a place to rinse dishes, cookware and eating utensils after meals. If it's cost-effective for you, use disposable cups, plates and utensils. You can also fill a recycled, half-gallon milk or juice jug with water and a bit of dish soap to wash your hands (and utensils) with a washcloth or paper towels after meals.

Re-use your plastic grocery bags for disposable trash bags. They can be dumped inconspicuously at grocery stores, strip malls, fast food places, rest stops, parks, and gas stations, to name a few. For recycling, receptacles can be found at apartment complexes, office complexes, grocery store parking lots, and city dump facilities in larger towns.

FOOD & WATER

Check with your local social services office to see if you qualify for food stamps. If you are not eligible, locate food banks near you by visiting http://feedingamerica.org and selecting your state. Some food banks don't care if you are a local resident or not; others will ask for a letter posted within 60 days showing that your address is in their service area. Explain to them that you are living in your car—everywhere is your address! If that fails, check to see if there is a food pantry (similar to food banks) in your area at http://www.foodpantries.org.

Fresh fruit and vegetables are incredibly cheap, fill you up, and keep you alert and healthy. Buy in quantity if you have enough space in the car, and the weather allows. For example, it's less expensive to buy a bag of apples than individual apples, but you wouldn't want to do that in 102-degree heat. If it's winter, or you're in a cooler climate, foods such as yogurt, milks and orange juice will store okay without ice or refrigeration for a few days. Cans of beans or tuna, peanut butter, dehydrated fruit, and cereals all hold up well in any weather.

Fast food and junk food are your worst enemies both financially and nutritionally when you are car dwelling. They are expensive, nutritionally bankrupt, and will not help you thrive under duress. Bread, fruits and vegetables, cheese and peanut butter are a bigger bargain, last longer, and are far healthier, and you can feed yourself inexpensively for several days with them. A bag of apples ($2.00), a bag of fresh carrots (.79 cents), canned veggies (2 for $1), a small jar of peanut butter ($4.00) and string cheese (5 for $1.00) won't even set you back $10. They will last longer, fill you up, and keep you healthier and more alert than dollar menus, sodas, potato chips, or other junk food, which will cost at least as much, and won't last more than a day.

If you have the capability to cook, bulk foods are cheapest. If you can't, ready made foods such as deli sandwiches will be easiest, but more expensive. Non-perishable foods and bulk food items are your wallet's best friend, as a little goes a long way. Sale items are also a good bet; check around online for sales circulars on Sundays, or look for in-store flyers.

If all else fails, dumpster dive behind restaurants (especially bakeries) and grocery stores. You will be positively stunned how much perfectly good food is thrown away (particularly unopened, packaged items) because it's either close to or just past its expiration date. Some places lock and guard their dumpsters like Ft. Knox, so smaller, independent grocery stores may yield better results.

As a last resort, you can stand outside a grocery store entrance and ask someone to buy something specific for you (i.e., peanut butter, trail mix, granola bars, etc.). This way you aren't begging for money, so the people you ask won't think you are going to blow it all on booze.

If you absolutely must have a hot meal, there are often free soup kitchens and church community meals you can attend.

Good: Community meals or soup kitchens, usually through churches or missions. Better: Food banks. Best: Food stamps.

As far as water is concerned, buy a few one-gallon jugs at any grocery or discount store, or re-use plastic juice jugs or soda bottles, and refill them from a potable (treated) source (e.g., the gym is an inconspicuous place for refills). One bottle is for drinking, one is for washing up and brushing your teeth, and the third is a backup for emergencies if you are not near a water source to refill the other two. This is important in the winter, in case you can't drive to the store or gym in snowy and icy conditions, and need water to survive.

If you don't have access to potable water, you can disinfect whatever fresh water supply you can find. If the source is from a stream or river, allow the silt and particulates to settle. If you have a camp stove, pour the water into a pot. Heat the water to a rolling boil, and let it boil for five minutes.

If you don't have a camp stove, or can't boil the water, you can disinfect it using bleach. Use 16 drops of household bleach to one gallon of water. Shake the water to mix it in well, and let it stand for 30 minutes. After that time, it should have a slight chlorine odor. If not, repeat the process again.

Documents

Put your car documents (car insurance, registration) in a separate envelope in the glove compartment, on top of everything else in there. This way, if you are stopped, you won't make the police officer nervous that you are fumbling around for a weapon. Keep your vehicle title separate from the car. Have a friend keep it for you, or put it in your storage unit. It is replaceable and only needed at the time you sell the vehicle, not during a traffic stop.

All vital documents such as wills, deeds, insurance policies, stocks and bonds, contracts, passports, immigration papers, social security cards, birth certificates, checkbooks and bank account numbers, credit card account numbers, birth, marriage and death certificates should be photocopied prior to living in your vehicle, and kept in a safe place in the vehicle (e.g., in a sealable, plastic bag under a floor mat, or behind seat cushions or covers). Keep the the originals in your storage unit, or stored with a trusted friend. Also, make a list of important phone numbers, and keep one copy with you, and another in storage.

If you are electronically savvy, scanning and uploading your vital paperwork to cloud storage is much safer than storing photocopies in the vehicle. Some public libraries have high-powered copiers that double as scanners. Or you can use the scanner feature on a friend's all-in-one printer if they have one. Purchase a USB drive (less than $10 for 8GB at most big box office stores) and scan the vital documents onto the USB drive as PDF files. Then upload the PDFs to Google Drive (an online document repository you probably don't know you already have, if you have any type of Google account, such as Gmail) for storage and safekeeping. Google Drive is especially helpful for storing your resume and references on, since you can access it from any computer, anywhere, if you need to pursue a hot job lead.

Employment

The cold and brutal fact is that without a job, you won't have perpetual income to pay for rent, gas or food. This means self-sufficiency is impossible. Unfortunately, in most cases, you'll have to earn and save enough money to buy your way out of your predicament. Sometimes, a small windfall such as an IRS tax refund can help, or a large windfall such as an inheritance. But those scenarios are out of the ordinary. Some places to find employment at all pay levels are online classified sites such as Craigslist or indeed.com; your local newspaper, local government websites (i.e., city, county, etc.), your local WorkSource office, and good, old-fashioned help wanted signs posted in business windows.

Having a job is a huge advantage for more than just financial reasons: it gives you a place to be during the day so you don't have to worry about the climate, and it also provides you with a place to eat and use the bathroom, and sometimes even shower. If you choose to work a graveyard shift, you have advantages over car dwellers with a day job. You can sleep during the day and no one will bother you, because people are at work and no one is looking for anything suspicious.

To be unemployed is essentially to be regarded as a leper. People will think you are lazy, or something is wrong with you, and won't want to help you.

Any employment, even marginal via something sporadic, will give you some respectability in the eyes of the people you encounter. If they see you struggling mightily even though you are employed, people will be more open to helping you.

If you live in a place where there is mostly a service and retail economy, where minimum wage prevails, you may have to seriously consider relocating to another city to find a decent-paying job to get out of your situation. Keep in mind that the better the job, the longer the hiring process tends to take. Enduring a three-month long hiring process while car living is one of the many types of vicissitudes that conspire to keep a person homeless longer.

Sometimes, luck plays a huge role. One former car dweller described the way he landed a job that freed him from a year of car living:

> "My life changed when I answered an ad in the *L.A. Times* for an editor/writer at a magazine...But the job went to someone else. About a week later, the magazine called me and told me the person they picked had quit, and asked if I was still interested.
>
> The week my unemployment ran out, and I had two bucks in my pocket, I got the job at the magazine. They had no idea I was homeless. For the first month, I worked at my job and slept in my car. After saving up money, I was able to move into an apartment less than two miles from where I used to sleep in my car."[56]

Finding A Safe Place To Sleep

Occasionally, something that works flawlessly in a big city will fail in a smaller town or rural area, and vice versa. That church parking lot you thought you could park and sleep in will get you towed in the city, and there's security patrols at that resort or hotel parking lot on the beach that you thought would be okay. Also, some places that may be unsafe in one location may be perfectly fine in another. It's not an exact science, because there's so many variables in each locale to consider.

Private vs. Public Property

In most places, it is illegal to camp or live in a vehicle on public property (such as libraries or city hall) or streets. Violators can receive anything from a mere warning, a citation, or towing and impoundment. The more inconspicuous you can be, the higher your success rate will be if you choose parking on the streets.

So that leaves private property, which includes strip or shopping malls, stand-alone businesses, college and university campuses and office complexes, among many other places. You generally need permission to park there, which is possible if you approach management or security and ask if you can stay overnight. There are pilot programs in cities such as Eugene, Oregon, where businesses will allow car dwellers who have been pre-screened (read: passed a background check) by social service agencies (or charities) to sleep in their parking lots. If you don't have permission, you can be subject to trespassing, with the requisite vehicle towing and impoundment.

Many office parks and complexes don't have security, and often have a few cars remaining in the lot at night. Yours may blend in, giving you a safe, well-lit, and quiet place to sleep. Don't do it if your car is the only one in the lot, as you will attract attention for looking out of place, particularly by police patrols.

Sometimes parking on private property can attract just as much attention as street parking. One Friday evening after cleaning crews in an office complex spotted me and called a tow truck in the highly-affluent area of San Clemente, California, I parked on a college campus in a smaller town farther north. It wasn't until the following morning that a security guard came on duty and approached me, just as I was getting ready to leave. (If you approach cops and security guards in a non-hostile, cooperative, and friendly manner, more often than not they will see you are not a threat, and it won't escalate into something truly unpleasant. See: Police)

You will have to decide which to use—public streets or private property— based on the circumstances of where you are, and assess the risk of being detected. Base your decision on the nature of the town and surrounding location, such as how much pedestrian traffic is around, and if your car blends in with other vehicles nearby.

Personal Safety & Vigilance

Hypervigilance and extreme forethought are necessary, especially for women. When it comes to safety, it is far better to have a cop knock on your window at 2 a.m. to tell you to move along, than to park in a place where there is no police presence and get attacked by a prowler.[57] Women should absolutely *never* park in isolated areas for *any* reason. It is far better to park and blend in where there's vehicle noise or other irritating but tolerable machinery, than to be raped and dumped in a ditch somewhere desolate where no one can hear or help you.

Always have a flashlight, cell phone, and pepper spray within reach while sleeping at night, as well as your car keys. A whistle is also helpful, and can be kept on your car keychain.

Pride keeps most people from telling friends and relatives about their situation, but concerns about police, and harassment from prowlers, are the top reasons people give for hiding their homelessness from others. Safety is a primary concern, because homeless people are often prime targets for crime.[58] Therefore, *never, ever* tell anyone, particularly strangers, that you are homeless or living out of your car, no matter how nosey and pointedly they ask, and especially if they aren't likely to help you. This is doubly so if you are a woman. If you feel you absolutely have to say something, tell them you are couch surfing or just passing through town on the way to visit relatives. Another reason for not discussing it with others, particularly in public or on a cell phone, is that you never know who is standing nearby and overhearing your conversation. Someone could easily follow you out of the library, coffee shop, or gym, watch you get in your car, and attack you then and there, or track you down later.

In rural areas or small towns, you may not have as large a risk of being a crime victim as in large towns or major cities. There is *always* a risk anywhere there is major drug activity, such as cities and towns near the Mexican border in the U.S., and bad neighborhoods in almost every city. If you are in an unfamiliar area, you can stop a police officer and ask them what areas of town should be avoided (particularly if you are a woman traveling alone). Once, I was supposed to stay overnight in a particular neighborhood in Phoenix, Arizona, but when I saw bullet holes in the stucco of several houses, and burglar bars on all of the residences, on the advice of the Phoenix police, I headed to Scottsdale to spend the night. Another time, in Seattle, I opened my car door and stepped on a used heroin syringe. Also in Seattle, I saw a guy hiding his syringe and other drug paraphernalia in a shrub in a public park. These are hopelessly obvious signs to move along and find another place to stay. In particular, women must be aware of and avoid areas frequented by male transients, such as railroad and industrial areas. Also, if you see gang graffiti or high crime area notices posted, go elsewhere. Any place that's vehicle accessible means you can be approached by anyone at any time.

Before bedding down, note the nearest cross streets, or even better, a landmark or an address number. That way, if you have to call 911, and they ask for your location, you can say, "I'm the blue Toyota behind the McDonald's on 47th Street," rather than "I don't know, I don't live here."

Successfully avoiding detection can depend on the type of car you drive. Obviously, you will be less conspicuous if you are living out of a late-model SUV or sedan, rather than a 1970s beater. Some people recommend a car cover. I don't, for two key reasons: 1) They attract attention because they are rarely used. Most people have garages or just leave their cars exposed. 2) You will attract attention trying to get in and out of the car with the cover as a barrier to your goal. As such, you also wouldn't be able to escape quickly in an emergency, either.

You should not be visible to passerby. Removable window covers and tinted windows are a great help, or you can cover yourself completely at night with a lightweight sheet or blanket.

Carry little to no cash; $20 or less. If you need more, use travelers checks. Credit and debit cards are easily replaced if stolen or lost by contacting your bank or credit union, and have limited loss and liability. Once cash is gone, it's gone. If you can afford AAA, join them, as they will be very helpful if you break down or your battery dies. They also offer travelers checks without the fees.

Location, Location, Location

Empty houses for rent or sale, foreclosures, and summer homes are the best locations to park and spend the night.   You can often park in the driveway if the house is not in a very busy subdivision. If it is, you can park on the street in front of the house.   You can do the same with summer homes in the wintertime in places that have seasonal populations—in the summer and spring, that same place is crowded and expensive. But in the off-season, they are almost deserted, so you will most likely be left alone.

Residential areas that are still under construction are a great place to spend the night. There are plenty of vacant lots you can park near or in front of, but avoid parking in driveways if the lot has one. Be sure to leave before construction crews arrive for work early in the morning. A residential area in a city near a main street can be good if you can find a parking space, and a permit or meter payment isn't required. Subdivisions are usually full of people walking their dogs or going for an evening stroll, so scout carefully before parking. The later you arrive, the better.

Contrary to popular belief, most WalMarts generally *don't* allow overnight camping due to local vagrancy laws, and a few bad apples who abused the privilege. But company policy doesn't ban it outright at *all* locations.[59] If you don't see a sign that says, "No Overnight Parking" at the entry to their parking lot, call ahead and check with the store manager to see if it's allowed. Due to being high violent crime magnets (rape, armed robbery, kidnapping), I highly recommend *against* sleeping overnight in WalMart parking lots (especially if you are a woman), as the company has shown it cares more about what happens inside its stores than outside of them.[60] If you do choose to overnight there, make sure you check out the surrounding neighborhood first; some WalMarts are located in seedy areas, which will put you at high risk. And don't be lulled into a false sense of security if you see surveillance cameras in the parking lot—they are not there for patron safety, or to prevent crime; they are there to keep tabs on union activists.[61]

You can also park in the lots of some hotels or motels if they don't have security patrols. Small, ten-room motels will get you noticed—and booted. A mid-sized hotel chain in a decent location (and at an off-season time of year) can work splendidly. So can smaller condo resorts. Larger hotel chain resorts in expensive areas (i.e., San Diego) tend to have security guards.

College or university campuses usually require a parking permit (a major revenue generator), and have security patrols. Libraries tend to lock parking garages after hours, and those that don't are a bad idea because police patrol the area, and a car there after hours is going to look suspicious. City parks often have drug or gang activity at night, which then attract the requisite police patrols.

Some rural roads on the outskirts of small towns and cities are a good bet if you can get far enough off the main road, and especially avoid the road shoulder. You don't want a drunk driver plowing into you at 3 a.m. in the rain and fog. Again, if you are a woman, consider your risk factor of being in an isolated area.

Casinos are also a good bet, because they are generally open 24 hours, but they can be noisy with all the coming and going of patrons. As far as church parking lots, don't park in the lot itself without permission; instead, park on the street in front of them, or across the street. Sometimes, depending on the size of the town, you can risk parking near or at city hall, if they don't house the police station there. Truck stops are a last resort, since they are very noisy, like most rest areas. Park near a building, rather than in the main lot, as your vehicle can be struck by sleepy truckers not expecting to see a car in their path.

If all else fails and you are too exhausted to drive to find a place, you may get away with a few hours stay in a convenience store or 24-hour fast food place's parking lot (or near one). Again, it will be noisy, but it will buy you some time and also give you a nearby restroom. The same holds true for rest stops (day only), truck stops, and even airport cellphone waiting lots if you are in a large enough city. Rest stops are okay (but noisy) during the day if you want a nap, but don't stay at rest stops during the night (especially on the West Coast), especially if they are rural or isolated.

If a campsite is your only option, avoid wasting gas by checking online sites for city, state, and federal parks ahead of time to see if they have entrance fees, showers and restrooms. I actually carry a hardcopy list of these in a plastic bag under the front seat—that's how important they are as a last resort. National Forests tend to have free campsites, or allow "dispersed camping" (a.k.a. boondocking), which means camping outside of developed campgrounds.

Once you find a safe place to sleep, the fundamental objectives are to arrive at your sleeping spot after dark, leave before sunrise, and not attract attention to your vehicle. During the summer, scout for a location during the day, and arrive after dark, which can be as late as 9 or 10 p.m. in northern latitudes. Leave by 6 a.m., so you aren't spotted by people walking their dogs or working an early shift. In the winter, it gets dark early (4:30-5 p.m.) in northern latitudes, so you can go to sleep earlier and leave earlier.

Never sleep in the same location two nights in a row, especially if your vehicle is conspicuous (e.g., out-of-state plates, beat-up old car, etc.) If you are staying in the same town for work, you can rotate your locations during the week, and leave town on weekends. Parking near old forest roads in the spring, summer and fall can be absolutely blissful. Most are closed in the winter.

Places to Avoid

Public school parking lots. Even in summer they have classes and staff coming and going. Office parks with security guards. Public (paid) parking spaces or garages. Some post offices, grocery stores, strip malls and hospitals have security. Ditto for shopping malls. Park in condos or apartment complexes only during a snowstorm; otherwise people will notice you and call management—or the police. A tow truck is sure to follow.

Kindness From Strangers: There's Always A Catch

People will sincerely offer to help, but thoroughly assess how well any offer of help fits your needs. Sometimes there are strings attached, and often the help is a temporary panacea that doesn't provide a long-term solution. This leaves you very vulnerable to people's whims, and boundaries of generosity. People can show genuine concern to begin with, and then dump you back on the streets when they see how complicated homelessness is, and don't want to deal with it anymore. So carefully consider what's being offered, and what ways things can go wrong and leave you worse off than when you started, before accepting help.

Fully understanding the stigma of homelessness, most of the time I didn't expect help from people I encountered, so I wasn't disappointed when there wasn't any forthcoming. A few women who approached me offered tangible help, such as money, or a place to stay, or a job lead. The few men I dealt with just acted concerned, and then passed the info along to others (usually women!) to try to get them to help instead.

There will be kind-hearted folks who will offer you a place to stay. There are varying degrees of this. One guy I had read about ended up as a paid caretaker of a vacation home the owners used three weeks a year. Another got to stay in a rental home from a friend's fire insurance settlement, because the friend chose to move in with his new girlfriend before the prepaid lease expired several months later. Others, including myself, have been a guest in the homes of complete strangers.

That's where you need to be careful—especially if you are a woman.

Some of them will ask you for a background check, which is fine. (Check your state police's website to see how to do this.) But don't assume that the people who invite you to stay are safe, kindly, or well-meaning just because they own a piece of property with a dwelling on it. Also, not all offers of help are benevolent—one sixty-something man offered me completely inappropriate rooming arrangements, and was stunned when I refused. A convicted felon offered to bring food and supplies to my car. He, too, was surprised when I refused.

So accepting help of a temporary nature that doesn't solve the core problem of homelessness can set you up for rejection and disappointment if things don't work out, and you find yourself back in your car again. A former roommate kindly housed me when I was running a fever for several days in forty-degree weather prior to a very high-level job interview. She was allergic to cats, and not keen on helping me out of my situation without a job. When I didn't get the high-level position, I was out on the streets again —the day before Thanksgiving.

Then there was the nice couple who took me in and spared me from ice, snow, and cold (which my ancient car is terribly ill-equipped for) for three weeks over Christmas and New Years. The Ben Franklin quote, "Guests, like fish, begin to smell after three days" proved true. After the novelty wore off, the tension of having another person in the house who was nothing like them began to build. I house-sat for them while they vacationed in Hawaii over New Years, and then left. It was a relief for both of us, I think, but particularly me, because their disorganized and chaotic family life was very jarring, compared to having been by myself in relative peace and solitude in the car for so long.

People are very reluctant to help if you don't have a job, because they are afraid you will become dependent on them, and cost them money. If joblessness persists, their fears aren't altogether unfounded. There may also be limits to which people are willing to help:

"In 2006, I met a homeless man who told me of his struggles trying to get off of the streets with the broken systems in place to help the homeless, and how they just weren't meeting his needs, though he was trying diligently to get into a better situation. He had posted an ad on Craigslist asking for job interview clothes.

We met, and I bought him some clothes at a thrift store, and got him a haircut. He was so moved by this simple kindness, that he teared up as he gave me a big hug. So many people ignore you when you're homeless, he said. I went on to take him to a few job interviews, and bought him a prepaid cell phone. He found work and became self-sufficient again relatively soon after that, but it was a drain on me, financially and time-wise."[62]

People can have benevolent intent to begin with, but they often don't understand that getting out of homelessness is a long-term process. They become frustrated when circumstances don't change overnight, and jobs don't just magically materialize out of thin air. Escaping from homelessness requires more than a bed to sleep in every night and three meals a day. People need jobs and real prospects for the future.[63]

Laundry

In the winter, you can often wear the same clothes more than once, because most of the time they are hidden under jackets and scarves, so no one will notice. In the summer, you will probably have to do laundry often to keep your clothes free of sweat and odor.

Laundromats are the the fastest way to eat up cash, especially if you have pets with you. Some homeless shelters have free laundry facilities, but the wait can be long. If you have a friend or relative who is amenable to letting you use their washer and dryer once a week, take them up on it. Keep your dirty clothes separate from your clean ones, or both will soon smell awful. Use a black plastic garbage bag for a laundry bag, as the amount of clothes you can safely fit in the bag is roughly the capacity of most standard washing machines.

Many campgrounds and truck stops have laundry facilities that are cheaper than a laundromat. Some hotels and motels do, too. You can also try to find an apartment complex large enough to have an unlocked laundry room. This may take some sleuthing, but the savings are worth it.

Buy detergent, dryer sheets, stain remover spray, etc., in advance and on sale, as you will get gouged for the smallest, one-load box of soap at a laundromat vending machine. Put detergent in smaller plastic bottles (such as water bottles for liquid detergent, or plastic zip bags for powders), if necessary, to take up less space in your car. You can use baking soda in the rinse water for fabric softener, as it's cheap (less than a dollar a box), very effective, and can be purchased with food stamps.

Clothes will dry faster if you toss three or four tennis balls in the dryer with them. You can get free tennis balls from most athletic clubs, as they set aside the "dead" balls from tennis lessons to be disposed of. Always make sure your clothes are completely dry (in summer you can finish drying them in the car if it's sunny and warm outside, and you keep the windows open to let air circulate), otherwise they will get moldy and smelly, and you will have to redo them.

If access to a washer and dryer is not possible, you can fill a five-gallon bucket with fresh water, and laundry (or dish) soap. Using this method, you can wash a handful of clothes at a time, agitating the contents by hand for several minutes to get them clean. After washing, dump the wash water and refill the bucket with clean water to rinse. Then, dump the rinse water, wring out the clothes and hang them to dry on the rope you use for your living space privacy divider, or if you're in a natural setting with some privacy (i.e., parks), lay them out on rocks or hang them from bushes to dry. If you're in a hot climate such as the desert Southwest, the clothes will dry very quickly in the car if you hang them as best as you can and keep the windows open. In colder climates, there's almost no getting around using a dryer, unless you want your laundry frozen stiff.

If you can't wash your clothes with a washer and dryer, or a bucket, you can always look for a creek, stream, river, or lake, and wash them there (provided you have enough privacy, and don't attract attention). Be sure to use biodegradable soap if you do. Clothes washed in natural settings tend to dry stiff, but at least they will be somewhat clean. If you're in a cold climate with snow nearby, you can wash your clothes in the snow, as the cold will help neutralize odors.[64] (Note that it will not remove the dirt, dust or stains; only the smell. And no, don't use fabric air fresheners to try to get rid of odor—all you are doing is spraying perfumed chemicals on your clothes, rather than removing the cause of the odor.) After snow-washing, you can place the clothes on the hood of your car to dry in the sun, and if there's no sun, the engine heat transferred to the hood from driving will help after you are parked, but it will take awhile. A better option may be to build a campfire and dry them nearby.

When washing your bedding, if you are in a stationwagon or SUV, it's a good time to clean the plastic liners underneath your bedding with some bleach on a wet washcloth. This removes bacteria, mold, and mildew generated by the condensation from your living space.

Mental Health

Car living on a road trip is a piece of cake, because you have something fun to look forward to, and a home to return to, when the journey is done. Car living when you have nowhere else to go is very, very different—it's an ongoing struggle, and it's very easy to fall into an abyss of hopelessness and depression. The experience of homelessness results in a loss of community, routines, possessions, privacy, and security.[65]

If you're unemployed, killing time becomes a focus, especially spending endless hours in parks and libraries, the last bastions of the poor.[66] As one former homeless man in England described it:

"The worst thing wasn't the cold. It was the long periods of having nothing to do. I watched life happening around me—people on their way to and from work, or meeting up with their friends—and I felt estranged from it, almost as if I was superimposed over it. I could see events unfolding in front of me but I felt so far removed from what was going on that I couldn't meaningfully interact with any of it.

I used sit around wondering how I had allowed myself to get into this situation, and why my life wasn't normal; not out of self-pity, but out of a genuine sense of bafflement..."[67]

The alienation is understandable, as your friends or co-workers will happily discuss the latest reality TV show developments (or other banal trivialities), while you're wondering where you'll park to sleep for the night, or where your next meal is coming from. Along with the lack of informal support networks, isolation and loneliness are common among homeless people. A third of homeless men reported that their only daily contact was with service providers, and more than half of homeless people said they had no family ties. Less than a third of homeless people spend time with non-homeless people, and almost 38% of homeless people said they spend their entire day alone.[68] But, in the words of one former car dweller, it's not hard to see why:

"I really couldn't make any friends. I'd either have to lie so they never discovered I was homeless...or tell them the truth, and they'd bolt for the door. The toughest times when I was homeless were the holidays. There was no one to hang out with, and the libraries and most stores were closed."[69]

Periodically feeling negated, devalued, forsaken, unwanted, abandoned, humiliated, alienated, rejected, and ignored will be inevitable. You will cry.

You will lose hope. As long as your nervous breakdowns don't last long, you'll be okay. You can't stand around and bemoan the situation for long anyway, because there's too much to be done to survive, and to try to change your circumstances. Know that the feelings will come and go in waves—and have the patience to wait for them to pass.

Many people zone out in front of the TV after work. This is hard to do in a car, because the flickering light from the TV (or computer or DVD player) will attract the attention of passerby. You don't really have the luxury of escape in car living, because all your time is focused on looking for ways out of the situation. Even then, you will have long stretches of down time, where nothing is happening, and staying in the car constantly (especially in winter), will drive you stir crazy. Try to keep up with the interests you had before you became homeless. If you have to mentally check out for awhile, in the summer, some parks and recreation departments have free outdoor movies. You can also borrow music and audiobooks that come with built-in players from the library.

As mentioned previously, when people find out you are homeless, their reaction isn't pretty. Know that it's their problem; you represent their worst fears, and they are reacting to that. For them to judge (and label) someone based on a temporary or short-term crisis, which is nothing more than a blip and an aberration over the span of a human lifetime, is absurd. The reality that society refuses to face about homeless people is that the majority of them are not in that situation through their own creation—they did not create the terrible economic policies and erosion of social safety net protections they are the direct victims of.

Sometimes when I was feeling down, I remembered Holocaust literature I'd read over the years, like Art Spiegelman's graphic novel series *Maus*, and concentration camp survivor Viktor Frankl's various works. Car living seems like a downright luxury compared to what those people were put through by the Nazis. It helped put the misery of the situation into some perspective, even if only an abstract one. I certainly had a lot more options available to me than people in concentration camps, and many of them made it through. I could, too.

One former car dweller wrote about his particular inspiration:

> "I checked out the shelters in downtown L.A., and they were overflowing and depressing. I knew if I ever ended up there I would never get out. I recalled an interview William Shatner gave. He said right after *Star Trek* was canceled in the late '60's, no one in Hollywood would hire him, and he had to go on the road and do dinner theaters. To save money, he said he lived in his car.
>
> I figured if Captain Kirk could pull that off, then so could I. I knew Los Angeles like the back of my hand. I knew where it was dangerous and where it was safe, so I decided to live in my car."[70]

The cycle of emotions when you are homeless usually follows a swing pattern between pain, hope, disappointment, and consolation. Each person responds differently. People with a religious background will use their faith for hope and inspiration in their darkest hours. For me, being non-religious, skeptical, and atheistic, I didn't go the spiritual route when things were tough. I knew there was no capricious sky daddy, or guardian angel who was going to to help me—I was totally on my own. Staying focused on my immediate needs ("I need gas in the tank", "I need a lighter pair of shoes", "I need a job"), staying alert, trying to make things happen, and living day-by-day produced far more results for me than any prayer, religion or faith could. But being non-religious didn't mean I didn't look for church resources to help. There just weren't very many in my area that have substantial homeless assistance programs. In a larger city (50,000+), it would have been far easier to facilitate parking permissions, showers, laundry, restrooms, and a hot meal from faith-based organizations.

So I based my mental approach on a Navy SEAL technique I had read about.[71] It utilizes the following steps to cope with extremely stressful situations:

1) Determine your immediate need, and focus or visualize it clearly. For example, "I need a place to go with my cat to get out of the cold for awhile" was one of my immediate needs one particularly frigid and windy day. I looked around and noticed an office building down the street that had few people in it, and a deserted lobby. I went inside with my cat in his harness, and sat on the floor in the hallway with him for half an hour to thaw out. No one came out or otherwise knew we were there.

2) Set microgoals. "I need to find a place to live" is not a microgoal, it's a macrogoal. "I need to make it four more days until my job interview" is a microgoal.

3) Positive self-talk intended to decrease anxiety. I didn't really use this one, because it feels a bit like trying to con yourself by repeating, mantra-like, "I can do this...I can do this...I can get through this..." But I *did* know I could hang tough and focus only on the short-term, having done that many times before in other circumstances. That, and knowing that the situation was temporary—even if temporary meant a couple of years.

4) Breathing to decrease anxiety. I knew from having read science magazines with articles about the subject that this technique would work; there was medical research to support the physiological effects of breathing to reduce stress and anxiety. This was probably the most helpful factor of the four, and something I'd practiced long before I began living in my car.[72]

So try to take things day by day, and moment to moment. It's all too easy to overwhelm yourself with a "When is this going to end?" obsession. Things can change in a heartbeat, or drag on for months or years. The wait is excruciating, like being adrift at sea with no wind in your sails for what feels like an eternity. It's the worrying about how soon your ordeal will end that will push you into the abyss. You have to take things one small step at a time, or you'll unnecessarily overwhelm yourself.

Money

Credit unions are *always* better than banks. Most of them have shared-branch capabilities, so you can go into most credit unions anywhere in the country and do your banking without fees, hassle, or having to open a local account. Also, if you accidentally bounce a check or overdraw, credit unions are more forgiving and will often waive the overdraft fees if you haven't made a habit of it. If you use a bank instead, check to see if there are branches in locations you plan to travel to, since many banks are regional and charge hefty fees for using other banks' ATMs.

If you are collecting unemployment, you are in a far better position than someone with no income, living off of meager savings. If possible, save more money than you think you'll need ahead of time. If you don't have a credit card, try to get one before you become homeless. It will save your life in many ways, such as giving you the ability to check into a motel during a snowstorm when it's not safe to be in a car, or to pay for unexpected car repairs or medical bills. Not to mention gas, where prices at the time of this writing are roughly $3.40 a gallon, and rising. You can always use a free credit counseling service to negotiate down the debt and interest with the credit card company once you get back on your feet again.

There's no time for sentiment or luxury during a crisis—heirloom furniture or jewelry are useless to hang onto when you need cash to survive. Check out pawn shops if you need immediate cash, or use eBay, Craigslist or other online marketplaces to sell your valuables if you have some lead time before becoming homeless. That way you won't be desperate to take the first (and probably lowest) offer that comes along.

Being homeless is time-consuming and expensive, as you have to do many of the same things that people with houses do on a daily basis, with all the requisite costs of living for items such as food, gas, etc. Shop at discount places or thrift stores. Most dollar stores have food and other essentials (i.e., first aid, hygiene, etc.) that you don't need to pay full retail for in grocery or drug stores. Many of them also carry food items. Never pay full price—clip coupons out of newspapers and buy items on sale. Some places, like food co-ops or smaller thrift stores, have a "free box" of donated items outside. Use GasBuddy.com to find the cheapest gasoline stations in your area. Cut down to bare essentials, and calculate in advance what you'll need on a weekly basis, and the associated costs. For example:

Storage Unit	$10 week
Food	$25 week
Laundry	$5 week
Gym Membership	$10 week
Gas	$25 week
Car Repairs	$10 wk (saving for oil changes/repairs of almost $500/yr)
Insurance/Tags/Fees	$10 week (saving up over 52 weeks)
Misc. (hygiene, clothes)	$10 week
TOTAL:	$105 week

So as you can see, this can easily eat up more than half of a $200/week unemployment check, or net pay from a $10/hour, part-time job. Plan and budget ahead as best as you can, and stick to the budget, because the money never lasts as long as you hope it will.

Can and bottle deposit recycling for cash is a problem, because you have to haul the cans and bottles to the recycling center, and you need volume to make the money worth the effort. At five or ten cents refund each, you'd need at least 100 bottles or cans to make five or ten dollars.

Donating blood (actually, plasma) is not as easy or cost-effective to do as it was in the pre-AIDS era. It's enormously time consuming, especially on your first visit, since they have to run all kinds of diagnostics to see if you can be a donor. It pays roughly $15 a visit (this will vary by region and demand), and almost always requires proof of residency and your Social Security card. It's a hassle and a last resort, but it is an option if you are desperate.

Real Change or other street newspapers in your area (see Appendix D) are a good way to earn money, be social, and stay connected.[73] And keep an eye on your car while doing so.

Since this book is about staying within the law, I strongly advise against shoplifting, even though the temptation will be great at times to do so. In 2008, I saw Kelly Reichardt's brilliant indie film, *Wendy and Lucy,* about a young woman trying to make it to Alaska from Indiana with her dog to find work in the infamous canneries. En route, Wendy's car breaks down in Portland, Oregon, and her troubles compound from there. Many of Wendy's problems stem from getting caught shoplifting food for her dog, even though she had enough money to pay for it. At one point, I went almost two months with less than $2 to my name. Knowing that if caught and arrested for shoplifting (highly likely, because I don't have any practice at it since childhood), I would never be able to pay bail or a fine, and would put my cat at risk of being locked in the car with no food and water until I could be released, was an extremely strong deterrent. Beg or borrow if you have to, but absolutely do not steal.

Pets

One of the reasons many people end up living in their cars instead of homeless shelters is because most shelters won't allow pets. And the shelters that do may not be near where you work and park to sleep. Having pets when you're homeless is a double-edged sword. Pets are the closest reminder of normalcy before you became homeless. They are great companions, and can really pull you out of yourself and momentary mental funks, because pets need to be cared for regardless of your mood, or what happened to you during the day. But caring for them can be a financial burden, and keeping them cooped up in a car while you work all day can stress them out considerably.

Most pets don't like cars because they associate them with going to the vet. Pets want one thing, and that's familiarity. Car living can be traumatizing to them because of all the different (and unfamiliar) noises and smells they encounter. So try to bring familiar essentials along, such as their usual blankets or bedding, and food and water dishes. It may be more practical, though, to use plastic dairy containers with lids for food and water, to prevent spills while driving, especially if space is limited in your vehicle. Bring pet food, a water bottle, bowls, cat litter pan, and a manual can opener for when the pop tab inevitably breaks off canned food. Bring a few pet toys, too, if you have the room.

Pets can snuggle with you under down comforters and sleeping bags in winter, but hot weather is an absolute non-starter. A Stanford University study demonstrated that even on relatively cool days (i.e., 72 degrees), the internal temperature of a car will zoom to 116 degrees within an hour. Keeping windows open a crack barely slows the rise at all. The bottom line is that your pet will die from heatstroke, period.[74] An additional problem in hot weather is keeping open cans of pet food from spoiling. If you have a job, you can store pet food in the break room refrigerator during the day. If you're unemployed, you'll need a mini-cooler with ice, or you'll have to buy food in costly small cans or pouches that your pet can consume within a single meal. Otherwise, in hot weather you'll have to feed your pet only dry food, and dietary changes can stress your animal out even further.

If you know your situation is temporary, and have the resources to do so, and your climate is cool enough, keep your pet with you in the vehicle (depending of the size of the pet, of course!). If you live in a hot climate, or work most of the day, it is a better idea to board your pet with a friend, relative or neighbor. If that won't work, place an ad on an online bulletin board such as Craigslist to see if you can find someone to temporarily foster your pet until your situation changes. Of course, you'll probably have to pay for food and care, but see what you can work out. If you're in a rural area, try to find someone with farm property—the pet can stay in a barn during the day. You have to do what's best for the animal—that's why the movie *Wendy and Lucy* was so heartbreaking. Only surrender the pet to a shelter (preferably one that is designated as no-kill) as an absolute last resort. A pet may be miserable living in a car, but it's far preferable to being euthanized.

Before becoming homeless, try to stockpile a lot of pet food on sale as far in advance as possible. Put only what you need in your car, and the rest in storage. This will keep you from overpaying when you run out and it's *not* on sale, as well as keep you stocked up if you are in areas not close to a store. Some food banks carry donated pet food, but it's rare so don't rely on it. Some large, independent grocery stores carry bulk, dry dog and cat food for around $.59 cents a pound.

If you absolutely can't afford any pet food at all, you can try the following: 1) Go to your nearest animal shelter or big box pet food store, and ask if they have dry food samples you can try. Pets can be finicky, and large bags of food can go to waste if the animal doesn't like it, so this is a normal item for them to have. Some smaller, local pet food stores have samples as well. 2) If you have a local dog park, you can ask an owner if you can have a small container of food; 3) If you're desperate, you can solicit passerby in front of a supermarket to see if they will purchase a few cans (or a bag) of pet food for you. 4) Another desperate measure is to dumpster dive behind pet stores, as some of them dump food that has damaged packaging, or is beyond the expiration date. Most donate those items to animal shelters, but it's worth a try.

Make sure you have all vaccinations up to date, and plenty of medication on hand if your pet needs any. Often, generics can be purchased for a fraction of name brands—ask your vet about it. Look for low-cost vet clinics for inexpensive vaccinations, or your local animal shelter. Animal shelters will often hold monthly clinics specifically geared toward cheap vaccinations (e.g., $20-$40 for a year's worth of shots). These low-cost clinics also have inexpensive microchipping services ($40 or less) that are a *must* if you are living on the road with your furry friend. Pets will bolt when scared or in unfamiliar surroundings, so chipping your pet greatly increases your chances of having it returned to you if the unthinkable happens and you are somehow separated.

Scan medical and vaccination records, as well a current digital photo to Google Drive (See: Communications) in case your pet is lost. Keep the originals in a safe place away from the vehicle, such as a storage unit, or even a desk drawer at work.

Absolutely keep your pet leashed or harnessed in unfamiliar areas at all times. If you are going to be spending a lot of time in one area, it will take a couple of weeks for the animal to recognize the sights and smells of your surroundings. Only then can some free-range be allowed, *but*, be careful, because other people may be out with their animals, and if yours isn't on a leash, it can invite trouble. If your animal doesn't have tags with your name and phone number on it, get a waterproof marker and write that information on leashes, harnesses and collars.

A dog in the car is an excellent crime deterrent, and a cat to curl up with can mean the difference between a stressful night or a tranquil one. And you never know—after a homeless man with a medical emergency was rescued because he attached a "need help" note to his dog's collar, and a local woman found the dog with the note and called police—having your pet with you could mean the difference between life and death.[75]

Physical Health: Medical & Dental Care, Medications & Vitamins

The life expectancy of homeless persons is 30 years less than for other Americans, and their rates of illnesses of all kinds are far greater than for others.[76] More than half of people experiencing homeless nationwide have no health insurance, and are typically unable to access the health care they need to stabilize and resolve their health issues, which prolong their homelessness. Serious illnesses like HIV/AIDS, diabetes, and tuberculosis are more common in homeless people than among the general population.[77]

Physical health conditions that require ongoing treatment—such as diabetes, HIV/AIDS, addiction, and mental illness—are compounded by homelessness, and therefore difficult to treat. Medication can require special handling, such as refrigeration or special storage, which can be difficult for homeless people to accommodate. Preventative care can also be difficult for car dwellers to access due to its prohibitive cost, so they may wait to seek medical care until a trip to the emergency room is necessary.[78]

There are few things worse than medical bills when you're already struggling financially, and living in your car to boot. There are four major mainstream benefit programs that can provide health care services for the car dwelling homeless:[79]

1) **Medicaid** – The public health insurance program for people with low income and limited resources. For a state-by-state breakdown of eligibility requirements, visit http://www.benefits.gov and http://www.benefitscheckup.org.

2) **State Children's Health Insurance Program (SCHIP)** – The public health insurance program for low-income, uninsured children 18 years of age or younger who do not qualify for Medicaid.

3) **Medicare** – The federal health insurance program for:
   - People age 65 and over, or
   - People under age 65 who are disabled,
   - And people who have end-stage renal disease (permanent kidney failure that requires regular dialysis or a kidney transplant).

4) **VA Health Care** – Health coverage for veterans (women and men) who:
   - Were honorably discharged
   - Served one day of active duty before 9/7/80
   - Served two consecutive years of active duty after 9/7/80
   - Were a National Guardsman or reservist brought to active duty by the President

In many circumstances, you will qualify for Medicaid. Services vary by state, but the federal government mandates coverage for the following when they are deemed "medically necessary":[80]

- Hospitalization
- Laboratory services
- X-rays
- Doctor services
- Family planning
- Nursing services
- Medical and surgical dental services
- Nursing facility services for people aged 21 or older
- Home healthcare for people eligible for nursing facility services
- Clinic treatment
- Pediatric and family nurse practitioner services
- Midwife services
- Screening, diagnosis and treatment services for persons under age 21

If you don't qualify for any of the above services, don't panic—you still have plenty of options. In larger cities and towns, some community service organizations offer free medical and dental clinics either weekly or monthly. These mostly mobile clinics are the best place to go if a prescription runs out, or you have other non-emergency medical needs. Call 2-1-1, or check with your local human services office, or ask staff at local food banks if any mobile clinics are available in your area. Call ahead to find out if the free clinics require proof of residency, or other documentation. For a directory of Health Care for the Homeless Clinics, visit http://www.bphc.hrsa.gov and look for the "Find a Clinic" box. Enter your city, state, or ZIP code to find the nearest clinic in your area.[81] Another free medical clinic database you can search by state or ZIP is http://www.freemedicalsearch.org.

If there are no free clinics, you still have options. You can inquire with private physicians or walk-in clinics about cash payment discounts and installment plans. Do *not* risk your health because of lack of money, because something that starts off small can be addressed inexpensively, while letting it go can cause the problem to snowball into something worse, making treatment more expensive. Nip problems in the bud as soon as you can.

If you are sick or injured, go to the nearest hospital emergency room (ER) for treatment if you are physically able to. Get treated and worry about payment later, as many hospitals will allow you to negotiate to reduce the final amount, or have charitable foundations to either write off, or cover all or the majority of the costs. If they don't, ask about reduced rates for cash payments, or monthly payment plans.

If you are injured or sick long-term while separated from your vehicle, it may be impounded. If you are at the ER receiving treatment, you can park your car in the hospital parking lot without it being towed. If you have pets with you in the vehicle, let staff know, so they can make arrangements to care for them until you are released.

If possible, stock up on prescription medications before you begin living out of your car. A 90-day supply of generics for around $10 from most drug and discount retailers, as well as many large-chain supermarkets, is an inexpensive option.[82] Take half-doses where possible on pain relievers, cough medicines, or other over-the-counter medications to make them last longer. *Do not* do that with critical prescription medications for conditions such as diabetes, asthma, etc.

Many pharmaceutical companies have programs that provide free medicine to people with low income and who are homeless. Visit the website http://www.needymeds.org to see if you qualify for free or low-cost prescriptions. Or contact the Partnership for Prescription Assistance, which helps qualifying patients without prescription drug coverage get the medicines they need for free, or nearly free. Visit http://www.pparx.org or call them toll free at 1-888-4PPA-NOW (1-888-477-2669) to see if you are eligible. You can also contact individual drug manufacturers, most of which have indigent patient assistance programs (IPAPs) to provide free medications; a list is available at http://www.edhayes.com/indigent.html.

If you have an emergency dental situation, and no money to pay for treatment, check if there are any free or sliding scale fee dental clinics in your area by visiting: http://www.freedental.org and search by state or by ZIP code. You can also sign up for free email alerts as soon as a clinic is scheduled in or near your area. Another helpful resource is http://www.freedentalcare.us.

It's enormously stressful being hypervigilant on top of being homeless. Tryptophan or melatonin (don't take valerian) can help you sleep at night. To counter stress during the day without drowsiness, a calcium-magnesium-zinc supplement can help. These supplements are available at most major discount grocery stores. If you can't afford them, ask a store employee in the vitamin department if they have product samples. Expensive L-Theanine can counter cortisol-related stress, and SAMe can counter depression. Please note that I am not a physician, and this is not medical advice, so don't sue me.

Another way to cope with and decrease the mental stress of homelessness is moderate physical exercise, such as working out at a gym, or simply walking around a local park. Exercise will take your mind off things, as your focus will be on physical exertion, rather than ruminating about things. It will also allow you to stretch out from being cramped in the car, and get the blood flow going after hours sitting in cafes (or the library) looking online for jobs. Exercise releases endorphins, and just thirty minutes a day can make a huge difference for your well-being.[83]

Police

Since homelessness is not a crime, during the day no one will really have much legal standing to bother you, even if you or your vehicle condition do raise an eyebrow or two. It's at night when the ubiquitous "no overnight camping" ordinances kick in that things can get dicey. City ordinances frequently serve as a tool to criminalize homelessness. Of 224 cities surveyed in 2005:[84]

- 28% prohibit "camping" in particular public places in the city

- 16% had citywide prohibitions on "camping"
- 27% prohibit sitting/lying in certain public places
- 16% prohibit loitering citywide
- 43% prohibit begging in particular public places
- 45% prohibit aggressive panhandling
- 21% have city-wide prohibitions on begging

In some areas, particularly in larger communities, police have much higher law enforcement priorities to deal with, such as violent crime, drug dealers, and drunk drivers, rather than bother with car dwellers. The only exception is if someone calls and complains about you; then, they are required to make contact and investigate. But in general, searching out and citing homeless car dwellers is not a very high law enforcement priority. In other cities, particularly in affluent areas (where you shouldn't be parked anyway, such as Tiburon, California, just northeast of the Golden Gate Bridge), the police will actively hunt you down.[85]

It is not a crime to be homeless, but in most communities there are specific laws and ordinances against overnight sleeping and camping, and living in a vehicle, especially on public property or streets. (Private property is not as much of a problem.) Automatically assume everywhere you go that city ordinances don't allow living in a vehicle on public property (parks, libraries, etc.) or the streets, and seek out places that either don't violate the ordinances, or where your risk of detection will be minimal.

You will invariably cross paths with the police at some point, and most probably while you are asleep. Have your car registration and proof of insurance all together in an envelope in the glove box (on top, not buried at the bottom), so you can quickly add your license to it when asked for your documents. Above all, cooperate. Though homeless people are pariahs, you are less of a threat to police than a drunk driver or drug dealer.

Many car living books and websites advise you to lie to the police about your situation, which is utterly ridiculous. The reality is that the police have heard every conceivable story you can possibly weave them millions of times over, and can probably tell them better than you can. They know their jurisdictions, and they know where homeless people in cars tend to sleep. They know what looks out of place, and have seen car dwellers while on their patrols long before you started doing it. So you will fool no one by lying. As long as you are not committing a crime, you have no reason to fear the police. Play it straight with them, cooperate, and you'll be surprised how willing they are to leave you alone, and sometimes even advise of a safe (or safer) place to stay within their jurisdiction, or another. (I was fortunate where I was living in my car, because there is a large amount of homelessness advocacy and awareness in the community, and sensitivity training among the police.) As long as laws are obeyed, and you're not causing a public nuisance, and you're cooperative, cops tend to be sympathetic, and sometimes even helpful.

Avoid alcohol at all times, because if the police suspect it, you will be subject to search and interrogation, and possible DUI. If you smell of it without a container, it will lead to further search and investigation, and you will be in trouble that could have easily been avoided. You need as much alertness as you can muster to survive and persevere through your homelessness, not unconsciousness or escapism through drugs and alcohol. Do not carry firearms in the vehicle with you unless you have the proper permits, which should be kept in the vehicle at all times along with your car registration and other important documents. If you are stopped and the officer inquires about weapons, tell him or her that you have a permit and a registered, legal firearm in the vehicle with you. Inform the officer of its exact location, and then follow whatever instructions the officer gives you.

Almost every police department will handle homelessness and car dwelling differently than another jurisdiction, just like individual officers will handle each encounter differently—the response of an officer in Dallas, Texas, may be way different than one in Redding, California. An officer's response can also vary greatly even from within the same police department. Much like speeding tickets, it's generally up to the responding officer's discretion whether you will be cited or not for violating the no overnight camping ordinance, or a similar one. Some officers would write their own mother a ticket, while others practically have to be forced to issue a citation. In almost every case, your license and registration will be run to do a warrants check to make sure you're not on the lam. If you're in the clear, usually you'll be asked to move along, and that will be the end of it.

Keep in mind that it's far better to receive a citation and go in front of a judge to explain your circumstances, and request that the charges be dismissed, than have a police stop escalate into something unpleasant for no reason at all. If you end up on the wrong side of a situation, and need free legal help, look online using the search term "free legal advocacy for homeless" for the specific city or area you are in, as laws and the availability of help vary by state. You can also check for legal services at http://www.lsc.gov/find-legal-aid and search by your state. See Appendix A in the back of this book for other free or low-cost homelessness legal service providers that may be able to help.

Sleeping Comfortably

The key to a good night's sleep in a car (as well as avoiding back injuries) is to sleep in more than one position, and preferably a reclining or horizontal one. Learn to sleep in a 'z' or 's' shape, and change your position frequently. Depending on your vehicle type, such as a sedan or coupe, you may have to fold the rear seats down and extend yourself into the trunk, provided you have room because most of your gear is stored in the trunk. If your rear seats don't fold down to let you extend into the trunk, and you have to sleep in the back seat itself, tuck the seatbelt clasps under the rear seat cushions. In a larger vehicle, such as an SUV or minivan, an inflatable mini mattress for kids, or inflatable camping pad or bed, may help if you are exceptionally uncomfortable; just be sure to buy a battery-powered inflator. Some car dwellers remove the back seats from their car, and use plywood and foam padding to create a level, cushioned surface, and stretch out into the trunk. If you don't have the technical know-how to do this, seek out someone who can inexpensively.

For SUVs, trucks and stationwagons, use plastic layers such as tarps or plastic drop cloths underneath your bedding to protect against dirt and condensation. This will also help keep the chill of the metal chassis away from you.

Before you arrive at your sleeping spot, move your bedding from the trunk to the back seat. The more you get in and out of your car once you arrive at your parking spot, the more likely you will attract attention. Lock yourself in the vehicle and roll down each of your windows one half to three quarters of an inch for ventilation, so that condensation doesn't build up on the windows, which is a dead giveaway that you are living in your car. Hang your privacy divider between the front of the vehicle and your sleeping area. Finally, go to the bathroom before you go to sleep, so you won't have to fumble around in the dark, half-asleep, to find your bucket.

Never wear earplugs, as it will dull your reaction time to problems or predators. You must be alert and on guard for cops and vehicle prowlers at all times. (Better a bad night's sleep from noise, causing you to need a nap during the day, than a crime victim.)

Storage Units

A storage unit is a car dweller's saving grace, as it allows you to access many necessities and other items that you wouldn't otherwise be able to keep in your car because of extremely limited space. It also saves money, because it keeps you from having to re-purchase items you need and already own, but don't have the room to keep with you. For example, you can store winter clothes in the summer, and vice versa.

Assume the worst—that someone will break into your car and take everything except the vehicle itself. Or that your vehicle will be towed and impounded. Then what will you do? Under no circumstances should you have valuables such as an iPhone, tablet, or laptop computer anywhere in your vehicle, not even the trunk. Those items are specifically what vehicle prowlers look for. Split up your clothing by putting half of it in storage and half in your car. Keep your phone on your person at all times, and put your laptop or tablet in storage and use the library's equipment. You'll have to anyway if something is stolen, or the car is impounded.

The downside is that storage can get very expensive (especially if renter's insurance is required to lease a unit), and be almost useless if you are a long way (more than an hour drive) from its location. If you can't afford a storage unit, pare down your belongings to a few boxes of the most *irreplaceable* items (important documents, photos, etc.), and store them with a friend, neighbor, co-worker, or relative. Write "If found, please contact <your email address>" on the outside of each box you store with someone else. That way, if for some reason the person you left the boxes with isn't the person who finds them (due to death, divorce, etc.), you can be contacted and your belongings can be returned to you.

Failing that, purge, purge, purge, because the more stuff you have, the more cluttered and cramped your car living space will be. The rule of thumb is if something is irreplaceable, such as photos, store it. If it's replaceable (furniture, cookware, etc.) get rid of it.

Some homeless people have managed to find a way to sleep in their storage unit, but I don't recommend it, even in desperate circumstances (i.e., snowstorm). If you are discovered, you will be in violation of your lease, which means you and your stuff will be evicted on the spot. Then, both you and all of your belongings will be out on the streets, with your problems compounded.

Store an extra set of car keys in your storage unit and with a friend, which gives you double the back-up in case you lock yourself out of the vehicle. Also store an extra storage unit key in a sealed envelope in your file in the storage unit manager's office. That way, if your keys are lost or stolen, you can still gain access.

If you keep your unit number and gate code in your wallet, put additional "dummy" numbers on both sides of the real code and unit number, so if your wallet is lost or stolen, a thief won't know which digits are real, and rob your unit.

5.   AFTER HOMELESSNESS

Re-housing can seem more difficult than climbing Mount Everest in light of everything homelessness brings, and in many ways it is. The economic system is completely rigged against the poor, and car living (a.k.a. "mobile homelessness") tends to climb whenever the cost of housing outpaces wages. According to an annual study conducted by the National Low Income Housing Coalition, 2005 was the first year on record that a full-time worker at minimum wage could not afford a one-bedroom apartment anywhere in the country at average market rates.[86] So another obstacle facing car dwellers is the basic presumption that if a homeless person lands a permanent job, he or she is on the road to self-sufficiency.[87]

Getting a Roof Over Your Head Again

Transitioning back into housing can happen several ways:

- You can live in your car long enough to save up first, last and deposit money to rent an apartment or house. Sometimes landlords will allow you to spread out paying the deposit over time, rather than requiring it all up front.
- Save up enough money to find a roommate situation. This will often cost far less than an apartment or house on your own, and will get a roof over your head for protection from the heat or cold. The down side is that you may have to deal with someone else's drama and issues, such as drug or alcohol abuse, which in many cases is worse than living in your car.

- Get on the waiting list for public housing assistance or vouchers. Often the waitlist is long, and families get priority. Still, in some cities it's a possibility.
- Allow perfect strangers to help you, but use discretion. [See: Kindness from Strangers]

Saving for a Place of Your Own

Consider that most affordable housing, should you find it, usually requires first month's rent, last month's rent, and a deposit before they hand the keys over to you. Basic math shows how hard this can be to attain:

Example 1- Assuming the 2013 Federal Minimum Wage of $7.25/hour

$7.25/hr x 40 hrs/wk=$290.00/wk gross
$290/wk x 4 weeks=$1,160/month gross
$290/wk x 52 wks/yr=$15,080 yr gross

Some people argue the minimum wage should be raised to $9 an hour. It's still not enough to keep up with the cost of living and inflation.[88] Here's what the numbers look like at $10 an hour, a dollar more than proponents are calling for:

Example 2 - If the Minimum Wage Was $10/hr

$10/hr x 40 hrs/wk=$400/wk gross
$400/wk x 4 weeks=$1,600/month gross
$400/wk x 52 wks/yr=$20,800 yr gross

Example 3 - Assuming $12/hr

$12/hr x 40 hrs/wk=$480/wk gross
$480/wk x 4 weeks=$1,920/month gross
$480/wk x 52 wks/yr=$24,960

And all of that is pre-tax money. So at a 30% tax rate in the examples above, those numbers net an income of $812, $1,120, and $1,344 per month, respectively. That's not going to improve your situation—that's going to either keep you right where you're at, or eventually put you in a worse place. How? Because if the average studio or one-bedroom apartment (or even roommate situation) is $500 per month, and they want a $250 deposit, that's $750 required up front to move in. That's 65% of the monthly income of Example 1, 47% of Example 2, and 39% of Example 3's gross income. It's even worse when you run those numbers for the net: 92% of Example 1, 67% of Example 2, and 56% of Example 3. No one can sustain themselves, let alone get ahead, with those disparities, especially when you consider other basic living expenses (food, gas, utilities, etc.) *and* the annual rate of inflation, neither of which I figured in above. The figures are depressing enough without them.

Federal Poverty Guidelines - 2013
(Source: Federal Register: January 24, 2013) [89]

Size of Family Unit	Lower 48 States and D.C.	Alaska	Hawaii
1	$11,490	$14,350	$13,230
2	15,510	19,380	17,850
3	19,530	24,410	22,470
4	23,550	29,440	27,090
5	27,570	34,470	31,710
6	31,590	39,500	36,330
7	35,610	44,530	40,950
8	39,630	49,560	45,570
For each additional person, add	4,020	5,030	4,620

So the federal minimum wage guarantees a 2-person family (e.g., single mother with one child) will be at 100% of the federal poverty level, even if that person works 40 hours a week, since $290/week x 52 weeks equals just

$15,080 gross per year.[90] And it doesn't matter that for many low-income people, their federal taxes will be refunded back to them because they don't make much money. They will wait up to a year to see it returned, when most need it immediately.

Critics will argue that a worker could simply choose not to accept a job at a particular wage, but in reality, a person on the edge of poverty does not have that luxury. People on the lowest rungs of the economic ladder are given a choice of either homelessness and starvation, or a lifetime of economic slavery from which there is little chance of emancipation.[91] Research clearly shows that it's a myth that the U.S. is a land of upward economic mobility.[92]

Roommates

Roommates are one of the worst ways out of homelessness for several reasons. The first reason is that you will have to deal with other people's problems on top of your own. Secondly, it can be difficult to adjust, because in the car, you had privacy and solitude, and didn't have to worry about other people's needs. Third, when you get tired of dealing with someone else's relationship, drug or alcohol problems (often all of the above), and decide that moving back into your vehicle is the sanest possible option, you will be accused of "choosing" your car living lifestyle. Finally, and most important, your roommate is the leaseholder with all the legal rights to your living space. This means you can be tossed back out onto the streets on a whim with essentially no recourse. So all of these considerations have to be factored into your particular situation. In general, it's safer, cleaner, and warmer in a house or building than a vehicle. Beyond that, you will have to decide what you can tolerate, and then have a back-up plan in case things don't work out.

Subsidized Housing

Subsidized housing, such as public housing or Section 8, is often the only housing homeless people can afford. Unfortunately, the government housing programs available today are not enough to meet the needs of all the homeless people in America—the average wait time for a Section 8 voucher in 2004 was nearly three years.[93] The reality of subsidized housing programs is that the waiting lists are long, and the bureaucracy and red tape to be accepted into the programs is strangling. Don't give up—take it one step at a time. There are case managers who can help walk you through the process step-by-step; it's what they are paid to do, so don't be afraid to ask for assistance. When you get frustrated, remember: you can't get called if you don't apply, and each day you wait adds one more day to your homelessness, and is one day longer you'll have to wait to get called when your name eventually does rise to the top of the list. Also, you don't have to take what's available when the time comes, as you might have other options by then. The idea is that you want as many options available to you in the shortest time possible.[94]

Although permanent housing is most likely your ultimate goal, gaining acceptance into a program may take awhile. A housing crisis can sometimes be solved in three steps: 1) Emergency shelter, 2) Transitional housing, 3) Permanent affordable housing. Resolution will vary depending on your circumstances and program availability. [95]

There is a nationwide database of low income housing that you can search for your area. Visit http://www.lowincomehousing.us. For rental assistance programs, visit http://www.rentalassistance.us. They list both government plans and nonprofit rental assistance organizations, but do not themselves provide direct monetary rental assistance.

After the Ordeal

The constant hypervigilance needed to live in your car, either short or long-term, can take it's toll on your nervous system. After you transition back to housing, be careful if you begin to suffer symptoms of Post-Traumatic Stress Disorder (PTSD). This can occur either shortly after, or up to a year or two after homelessness. Symptoms include re-living the trauma, avoiding things that remind you of the trauma, or constant anguish or anxiety.[96]

It's natural to have some of these symptoms after a dangerous event. Sometimes people have very serious symptoms that go away after a few weeks. This is called acute stress disorder, or ASD. When the symptoms last more than a few weeks, and become an ongoing problem, PTSD might be the cause. Some people with PTSD don't show any symptoms for weeks or months.[97] If you are unsure where to go for help for PTSD, ask a doctor. Others who can help are:

- Mental health specialists, such as psychiatrists, psychologists, social workers, or mental health counselors
- Health maintenance organizations
- Community mental health centers
- Hospital psychiatry departments and outpatient clinics
- Mental health programs at universities or medical schools
- State hospital outpatient clinics
- Family services, social agencies, or clergy
- Peer support groups
- Private clinics and facilities
- Employee assistance programs
- Local medical and/or psychiatric societies

You can also check online for referral information. An emergency room doctor can also provide temporary help, and can tell you where and how to get additional and long-term help.[98]

Reintegrating with society again can be difficult, because your perspective is irrevocably changed. You're not like other people anymore, and you're never going to be like them again. You will be a completely different person, and can use your experience and understanding to help others in a similar situation.

6.   ADVOCATING FOR CHANGE

The best way to end homelessness is to prevent it, and opinion polls show that the majority of Americans are in favor of it.[99] But vigorous advocacy is needed, and new policies must be implemented to address the fundamental causes of homelessness:[100]

- Lack of affordable housing.
- Lagging incomes - Incomes for the poorest Americans have not kept pace with rising housing costs, and millions of workers are shut out of the private housing market.
- Slashed services and government assistance.

Asked to identify the top actions needed to reduce homelessness, 93 percent of the cities surveyed in the *U.S. Conference of Mayors 2011 Status Report on Hunger & Homelessness* called for providing more mainstream assisted housing (i.e., vouchers) and 78 percent called for more, or better-paying, employment opportunities.[101]

Lack of Affordable Housing

The generally accepted definition of affordable housing is when a household pays no more than 30 percent of its annual income on housing. Families paying more than that are considered cost burdened, and may have difficulty affording necessities such as food, clothing, transportation, and medical care. It is a significant hardship for low-income households, as it prevents them from meeting their basic needs.[102]

The National Low Income Housing Coalition (NLIC) publication *Out of Reach* captures the gap between wages and rents across the country.[103] For each state, it estimates the full-time hourly wage that a household must earn to afford a decent apartment at the HUD-estimated fair market rent (FMR), while spending no more than 30% of income on housing costs. The 2013 housing wage is $18.79, exceeding the $14.32 hourly wage earned by the average renter...and greatly exceeding wages earned by low income renter households. The study underscores the challenges facing the lowest income renters: increasing rents, stagnating wages, and a shortage of affordable housing. The urgent solution to these issues is clear: expanding the supply of affordable housing units, dedicated to the lowest income renters.[104]

The Census Bureau's 2011 American Community Survey showed that there are just 30 affordable and available units for every 100 households with an income at or below 30% of the area median income.[105] To help the supply catch up with the demand, a promising solution comes from the NLIC:

> "Enacted in 2008, the National Housing Trust Fund (NHTF) was created to address the acute shortage of rental housing the lowest income people in the U.S. can afford. Unfortunately, it has never been funded...
>
> If funded, the National Housing Trust Fund would provide permanent, dedicated funds for the production, rehabilitation, preservation, and operation of rental homes, at least 75% of which must be affordable to extremely low income households, and up to 25% serving very low income households.
>
> The National Low Income Housing Coalition calls for funding with savings gained from modifications to the mortgage interest deduction. Converting the current tax deduction to a 15% non-refundable tax credit, and reducing the size of a mortgage eligible for a tax break from $1

million to $500,000, would save the federal government almost $200 billion over ten years. Not only will these changes expand the number of low and moderate income homeowners who get a tax break, but it would provide enough funds to create millions of affordable rental homes for extremely low income households.

It is possible to end homelessness and assure real housing stability for the poorest American families without increasing federal spending, but instead using federal housing subsidies in a fairer, more efficient way.[106] Each year the federal government fails to fund the National Housing Trust Fund is another year that the shortage of homes for the lowest income Americans grows. This shortage places more poor families at risk of homelessness."[107]

So until the core, fundamental causes of homelessness can be eliminated, stop-gap measures such as providing eviction prevention services (which include rent subsidies, assistance with utilities, case management, or mediation with landlords, etc.), will continue to be the most effective ways of keeping individuals and families in their homes.[108]

Low Wages & Income Inequality

The increase in income inequality is shown by the fact that in the past three decades, high-wage workers have seen their paychecks grow, while median and low-wage workers have not.[109] In an era of low wages and high unemployment, it is pointless to continue funding programs to help people find the scarce jobs that are available, that won't pay a living wage, and will keep workers exactly where they are economically—or worse off.[110] The efforts would be better focused on reforming and instituting a fair and equitable economic system instead.

One out of every three families are now considered "working poor." Even though the overall number of people returning to work during the recovery has increased, the fastest-growing jobs have been in the lower-wage service sector. These lower-wage jobs represented nearly 60 percent of the jobs gained in the recovery of the past two years.[111] Many middle-wage jobs have simply disappeared.[112]

On February 12, 2013, President Obama declared in his State of the Union Address that "in the wealthiest nation on earth, no one who works full-time should have to live in poverty"—effectively calling for an increase in the federal minimum wage from its current level, $7.25, to $9.[113] The public appears united in support of Obama's proposal—71% of the population is in favor of the bump to $9, according to a Pew Research Center poll, while politicians, and economists, to a lesser extent, remain divided.[114] The brutal fact is that $9 isn't a living wage, either. The federal minimum wage in 2013 would be $10.67 if it had kept up with inflation over the past 40 years.[115]

Recently, in a number of high-cost communities, organizers and citizens have successfully argued that the prevailing wage should reflect a rate required to meet minimum standards of living. In response, MIT developed a living wage calculator (based on the most current census data) to estimate the cost of living in each state. The calculator (http://livingwage.mit.edu) lists typical expenses, the living wage, and typical wages for the selected location.[116]

Critics argue that a higher minimum wage will discourage companies from hiring, and that most low-wage employers are small businesses that are still struggling in a weak economy.[117] In reality, studies have shown that the majority of all low-wage workers (two thirds) are actually employed by large corporations, so raising the minimum wage won't harm businesses. And those large corporations are enjoying strong profits *above* their pre-recession levels, and are sharing them generously with their top executives and shareholders, rather than their employees.[118]

"The further that people fall behind, and the lower the minimum wage is, the more government subsidizes these low-wage workers," says Congressional Representative George Miller (D-Calif.). "We subsidize them with food stamps, and we will be subsidizing them with health care...I appreciate everybody thumping their chest about how they're independent, free-enterprise businesses, [but] they just want a government subsidy to pay the wages of their workers."[119]

Slashed Budgets & Bureaucracy: An Enemy of Help

Tax cuts for the wealthiest Americans and multinational corporations are lost revenue. As a result, social safety net programs are slashed, since there's less money to pay for them. Cutting taxes on the wealthy and large corporations increases income inequality and reduces funding for education, health and human services, and public safety.[120] It's a revenue problem (not a spending problem, as is often claimed by critics) that could easily be remedied by Congress. But there's no political will to do so, since the rich buy political influence.[121]

The mostly nonprofit providers of social services for the homeless are known as Continuum of Care (CoC) providers. Since community response such as church volunteerism can only go so far to help the homeless, the mission of continuum of care providers is to secure federal, state and local money to provide services that deal with the end result of homelessness, rather than prevention. Addressing and solving the root causes of homelessness is not their job, mission or focus, since continuum of care means interrelated and connected ranges of services and providers. What a service-heavy focus does is create a costly bureaucracy to administer it, a major obstacle homeless people avoid. It also siphons funds away from addressing the problem directly, such as building more affordable housing.

The data at the local, state, federal and international levels all reflect the same root causes of homelessness. Yet the local councils and committees in existence to specifically address homelessness still continue to ignore this data, and instead focus heavily on providing services (shelters, day use centers, etc.) instead of prevention. This is akin to having a dead battery in your car, and changing a tire to fix it. At the end of the day, people need homes, period.

Soup kitchens and shelters are the traditional ways society has looked after the homeless. But homeless advocates argue that making sure people can continue to afford housing is the central issue.

"Services not connected to housing do little good," says Larry Haynes, executive director of Mercy House in Orange County, California. "Pancake breakfasts provided by the middle and upper class make people feel better, but where are the pancakes the next day?"[122]

To be clear, services *do* play an important role, as no one wants to see anyone starve, or die of exposure from the elements from living in places not meant for human habitation. But they are only part of the overall solution, as services that don't focus exclusively on getting roofs over the heads of the homeless will never be the solution itself. So why are the committees, councils and politicians ignoring the core causes of homelessness?

1. Homeless people don't vote. As a non-vocal constituency in a political world where "squeaky wheels" get the proverbial grease, the homeless constituency is invisible. Homeless people also do not have time to advocate for their needs, because almost all of their time is spent on basic, day-to-day survival.

2. Almost all of the people who are members of the committees and councils are not, nor have they ever been, homeless. So these representatives and policy makers are making decisions for a population they are not part of, nor fully understand the needs of. Though their data clearly shows the direct causes of homelessness, they ignore it, and opt for providing services to deal with the result instead. This is partly due to the fact that service providers tend to be overrepresented on the committees. Homeless people are

heavily underrepresented on the committees for the reasons outlined above.

3. Companies (and their lobbyists and shareholders) will get angry and vocal (see: "squeaky wheel" above), and claim that increased wages will kill jobs and growth. The reality is that the current system of an unfair tax code, free trade, and overseas outsourcing of manufacturing jobs already does a far better job of that than any increase of workers' wages will. In fact, studies show that higher wages lead to increased economic growth.[123]

4. Money buys influence. On top of being invisible and having no voice, homeless people have no money. So they don't have lobbyists and campaign contributions to influence politicians to write laws in their favor. (For a general price list of what it costs to be heard in Washington D.C., read *Forbes* magazine's excellent article "Hey! Want to Buy Some Influence?")[124]

Politicians know all of this, so their staff will dismiss, ignore or stonewall you. Persist anyway, because there are a rare few who will listen, and you need to find them and work with them. The most empowering thing anyone can do, homeless or not, is speak up—relentlessly. Attend the meetings and ask the policy and decision makers tough questions, such as:

1. How are the homeless better off for the fact that your committee (task force, council, etc.) exists? How have you made their lives better than they had been before you were convened?

2. What tangible, quantifiable specifics and evidence can you provide to support your assertions of success? (e.g., A Safe-Place-To-Park program was instituted in conjunction with local businesses within the last year, and more than 81 people have utilized the program.[125])

3. What are your future plans, including specific goals, to continue to address this issue?

4. What is the ultimate outcome, and how do you intend to achieve it? Who do you intend to engage and enlist to accomplish it? How will you fund your solutions?

Don't let them snow you, and don't let them off the hook. At the end of they day, they get a paycheck, and have a home to go to whether anything gets done to help you—or not. You don't have that luxury.

Ten-Year Plans to End Homelessness Don't

The ten-year plans to end homelessness, written and adopted by many cities across the country within the last decade, are an abysmal failure for most of the reasons already outlined. While broadly identifying and addressing the core causes of homelessness, they come up terribly short on specific solutions. Unfortunately, the groups often end up surrendering to the problem, and ultimately build more and more shelters, instead of staying focused on addressing the core issues of homelessness. The city of Seattle recently admitted as much:

> "A higher-than-last year count of the homeless in King County underscored a change in funding priorities for the Committee to End Homelessness. Permanent housing is not keeping up with the need, so they are moving toward more emergency shelter space instead.
>
> The increase underscores what advocates for the homeless have known for years: The 10-year plan is not keeping up. The countywide plan's original vision was to build so much permanent, affordable housing that more emergency shelters would not be needed, but that hasn't worked.
>
> So this week, as volunteers prepared to do the annual overnight count, the Committee to End Homelessness adopted a new strategy: putting government money toward emergency shelter in addition to permanent housing."[126]

"In the past, our homeless system did not do much about housing except offer temporary shelter," says Nan Roman, executive director of the National Alliance to End Homelessness.[127] So while the ten-year plans are outlining the right strategies (e.g., build more affordable housing), they are not always setting clear numeric indicators, establishing timelines, identifying responsible bodies, and identifying funding sources for each strategy.[128] So more temporary shelters are built, and the cycle of failure repeats.

If Nothing's Changed, Nothing Changes

All of the issues are connected, and they affect you whether you have a home, live in your car, or on the streets. By doing something, something may change. By doing nothing, nothing will change. And given the core structural problems with the American economic system, things are sure to get worse for *everybody*, homeless or not, before they get better:

> "...Washington's actions could prove fatal. Barring wholesale changes in policies that are undermining the future of all but a few...the coming years will be grim. While there will be ups and downs in the economy, the future for middle-class America, along with the working poor who hoped to achieve that status—and in years gone by, would have—is over for tens of millions. As for the long-held mantra from the 1950s on, that children will enjoy a better life than their parents, only the delusional believe it today. Virtually no one says it."[129]

> "...Where once we were told, over and over, that anyone could move up the economic ladder, now that movement is, with some exceptions, down. It's going to continue in that direction with a vengeance until all that's left is the upper end of what once was a thriving, broad-based middle class. Everyone else will be toiling on a treadmill. The working poor, instead of moving up, will spend their lives like

hamsters on a wheel, mindlessly running round and round. "Retirement" will be a quaint term in the dictionary."[130]

You can either escape from or change the system, because to do nothing is to perpetuate it. As one former car dweller put it:

"Keep in mind: That woman who can't afford to see a doctor is someone's sister. That kid wandering the streets is someone's daughter or son. That homeless guy who was on the streets wrote the words that you are reading right now.

If you have never contacted a Congressman or Senator in your life about anything, please do it right now. Don't wait for someone else to do it. They are not going to. It's up to you. Don't wait for someone else to do it; they're busy watching TV. It's up to you."[131]

There are still people out there who care, who still believe in their system, and desperately want things to change. Seek them out.

There are also still good politicians out there, who care deeply, and who want to do the right thing—they're just outnumbered right now. And they are well aware that there are people who are walking away with unprecedented wealth, thanks to rigged economic, legislative and legal systems—all at your expense.[132] They know about the perks, breaks, giveaways, and pork the lobbyists slip through the legal loopholes to enhance their corporate benefactors—to your great detriment. They see it and loathe it as much as you do. They know the fix is in, and that it takes time, effort, education of the public, and enough people to change the systemic rot. So they fight back, one procedural rule change, one amendment, one policy, and one vote at a time.

What will you do?

APPENDIX A - ADDITIONAL RESOURCES

If you don't have Internet access, or if you need help or have questions, visit your local public library and ask a librarian to help you.

Information and other resources for people seeking assistance are listed by category below.[133] You can also visit the Homelessness Resource Center at http://homeless.samhsa.gov. Additionally, the U.S. Department of Housing and Urban Development (HUD) website provides resources at http://www.hud.gov. Look on the page where it says, "I Want to Find", and click on "Homeless Resources" from the list.

Child Care

To find local child care, contact Child Care Aware, toll-free, at 1-800-424-2246, or visit http://www.childcareaware.org. You can also visit http://www.nncc.org/states/stateindex.html and select your state to find programs in your area. For additional information on other child care issues, visit http://childcare.gov.

If you need help to pay for child care, assistance is available to eligible families through state agencies that administer Federal Child Care and Development grants. Contact the agency in your state directly for eligibility information and how to apply for assistance by visiting http://www.acf.hhs.gov/programs/occ/resource/ccdf-grantee-state-and-territory-contacts.

If you don't have Internet access, call the Head Start Information and Publication Center toll-free at 1-866-763-6481. To find a local Head Start or Early Head Start program to contact in your area, use the online national search tool at http://eclkc.ohs.acf.hhs.gov/hslc/HeadStartOffices. Contact the listed programs closest to your community, even if they are some distance away, as they are the main program offices which can tell you if there is a Head Start center closer to your area. Many of the organizations operate additional Head Start centers that are not listed, so there may be a program closer to your home than it appears.

Child Support

Child support advice for single mothers is available from the US Department of Health and Human Services (HHS). Call their hotline at 1-877-696-6775.

Dental Care

For a listing of free or sliding scale dental clinics, visit http://www.freedental.org, or http://www.freedentalcare.us.

Education

For help enrolling your child in school, call the National Center for Homeless Education at 1-800-308-2145. You can also visit their website at http://www.serve.org/nche, or email them at homeless@serve.org.

Emergency Assistance

For a listing of resources in your community, call United Way's First Call for Help by dialing 2-1-1. They are also on the Internet at http://www.211.org. Also visit http://www.nationalhomeless.org/need_help/index.html.

Employment

For information about jobs, training, and career resources, call 1-877-US2-JOBS (1-877-872-5627), or you can visit the American Job Center website at http://www.servicelocator.org/onestopcenters.asp.

Food

Food Stamps & Food Banks:

- ***To see if you're eligible*** for SNAP (food stamps) benefits *before* contacting your local benefits office, use the pre-screening eligibility tool here: http://www.snap-step1.usda.gov/fns

- To find out ***how to apply*** to the SNAP (food stamps) program: http://www.fns.usda.gov/snap/applicant_recipients/apply.htm. For toll-free, state-by-state SNAP information hotlines, visit http://www.fns.usda.gov/snap/contact_info/hotlines.htm.

- When you're ***ready to apply*** for food stamps, contact your local office.   To find the office nearest you, visit the website http://www.fns.usda.gov/snap/contact_info/hotlines.htm   and click on your state.

If you don't qualify for food stamps, to locate a food bank or food pantry in your area, visit http://feedingamerica.org/foodbank-results.aspx. You can also visit http://www.foodpantries.org.

School Lunch Programs:

- http://www.fns.usda.gov/fdd/programs/schcnp/pfs-schcnp.pdf
- www.fns.usda.gov/fdd/contacts/sdacontacts.htm

This National School Lunch and Summer Food Service Programs website gives details on how children in homeless families may be eligible for school lunches, school breakfasts, and meals during summer school break. The second link gives a state-by-state listing of contacts for the program, since it's administered at the state level.

Women, Infants, and Children (WIC) Program:

- http://www.fns.usda.gov/wic/aboutwic/wicataglance.htm

Pregnant and nursing mothers who are homeless, and children up to five years of age may be eligible for the Special Nutrition Program for Women, Infants, and Children (WIC). The WIC program can be a useful resource for food staples such as bread, milk, cheese, and juice.

Government Programs & Resources for the Homeless

To find government benefits that you may qualify for (i.e., Medicaid, Social Security, etc.), call the federal information line, toll-free, at 1-800-333-4636 (1-800-FED-INFO), or visit http://www.benefits.gov.

To find homeless service providers who can help you in your state, visit: http://homeless.samhsa.gov.

Health Care

- For free or low cost health clinics by state, visit http://www.needymeds.org/free_clinics.taf

- For a directory of Health Care for the Homeless clinics, visit http://findahealthcenter.hrsa.gov/Search_HCC.aspx. Type in your ZIP code, and click the "Find Health Centers" button for your nearest location. These centers provide care, even if you have no health insurance. You pay what you can afford, based on your income.

Services provided include:

1. Checkups when you're well
2. Treatment when you're sick
3. Complete care when you're pregnant
4. Immunizations and checkups for your children
5. Dental care and prescription drugs for your family
6. Mental health and substance abuse care if you need it

- U.S. Department of Health and Human Services, Centers for Medicare and Medicaid Services: http://www.cms.gov.

- Search by state for free or affordable dental clinics in your area. Visit http://www.freedental.org or http://www.freedentalcare.us.

- Search by state or ZIP for more free medical clinics at http://www.freemedicalsearch.org.

Housing

For information about housing programs and vouchers, contact a homelessness assistance agency in your area. Go to the website http://portal.hud.gov/hudportal/HUD?src=/states and click on your state. For a housing counseling agency near you, call HUD at 1-800-569-4287.

Visit http://www.lowincomehousing.us, or the Public Housing Network website at http://www.publichousing.com, and search by state to find low income housing all across the country.

For rental assistance programs, visit http://www.rentalassistance.us. They list both government plans and nonprofit rental assistance organizations, but do not provide direct monetary rental assistance.

Legal Aid

Free or low-cost legal assistance and services are available from the following:

- http://www.lsc.gov/find-legal-aid
- http://www.ptla.org/legal-services-links
- http://www.lawhelp.org/find-help/
- http://www.ptla.org/pro-bono-links

Libraries

To find the nearest library in your area so you can use the Internet, or just to get out of the cold, visit this website and type in your ZIP code:

- http://www.servicelocator.org/Libraries.asp

You can also visit http://www.publiclibraries.com to view a city-by-city listing for your state.

Prescriptions

- For free or low-cost prescription information, visit http://www.needymeds.org/indices/faq.htm

NeedyMeds is an information source, *not a program to sign up for*. They list programs that may provide assistance, and you apply directly to those programs. NeedyMeds doesn't process any applications, determine eligibility, or supply medications. Each program has its own application. You can find them by clicking on a drug name under Brand Name drugs, or Generic Name drugs. If your medicine is not listed, there are other options:[134]

1. Check back on NeedyMeds regularly. The programs change often as drugs are added and dropped, dosages change, and new programs are created.
2. Look for Patient Assistance Programs (PAPs) for all your medicines.
3. Use the NeedyMeds Drug Discount Card to see if you may be able to obtain a lower price for medication.
4. Look for other types of assistance on the NeedyMeds website:
   - **Diagnosis-Based Assistance** lists programs that provide a wide range of assistance for the costs of specific health problems.

- **Government Programs** are government-sponsored programs in each state that provide health care assistance.
- **Other Drug Discount Cards.** There are three categories: drug company discount cards, drug company discount cards for Medicare Part D enrollees, and state discount cards.

- For additional information on free or discount prescriptions, call 1-888-477-2669 or visit http://www.pparx.org.

Social Security

- https://secure.ssa.gov/apps6z/FOLO/fo001.jsp
- If you don't have Internet access, you can reach Social Security by calling 1-800-772-1213

If you live in the United States, for information and directions to the Social Security office that serves your area, visit the website above and enter your ZIP code and click on the "Locate" button. You'll get information about your local Social Security office, and other agencies in your area that may be able to help you.

If you call 1-800-772-1213, you can use the automated telephone services to get recorded information and conduct some business 24 hours a day. If you cannot handle your business through the automated services, you can speak to a Social Security representative between 7 a.m. and 7 p.m., Monday through Friday. Generally, you'll have a shorter wait time if you call after Tuesday. If you are deaf or hard of hearing, call the toll-free TTY number, 1-800-325-0778, between 7 a.m. and 7 p.m., Monday through Friday.

Substance Abuse

To search for free or low cost addiction treatment centers, visit http://www.freeaddictioncenters.com. For treatment centers that are free, affordable, discounted, low cost, sliding scale or Medicaid-based, call 1-800-

780-2294 to speak with a drug or alcohol counselor, or visit http://www.freetreatmentcenters.com and search by state.

Unemployment Benefits

To find out where and how to file for unemployment benefits, visit the website below and select your state from the list.

- http://www.servicelocator.org/UI_Filing_Assistance.asp

Youth

The National Runaway Hotline: Call 1-800-RUNAWAY or visit http://www.1800runaway.org

Runaway and Homeless Youth Programs:

- Basic Center Program:
  http://www.acf.hhs.gov/programs/fysb/content/youthdi
  vision/programs/bcpfactsheet.htm
- Transitional Living Program:
  http://www.acf.hhs.gov/programs/fysb/content/youthdi
  vision/programs/tlpfactsheet.htm
- Street Outreach Program:
  http://www.acf.hhs.gov/programs/fysb/content/youthdi
  vision/programs/sopfactsheet.htm

APPENDIX B - HELP FOR SPECIFIC TYPES OF HOMELESSNESS

Domestic Violence Victims

An unfortunate reality is that the majority of homeless women living in cars are victims of domestic violence.[135]   Among families, it is the third leading cause of homelessness.[136] Survivors of domestic violence are often isolated from support networks and financial resources by their abusers.   As a result, they have trouble finding apartments because they may lack steady income, or have poor credit, rental, and employment histories.[137] They also suffer from anxiety, panic disorder, major depression, and substance abuse.[138] Because of these considerable barriers, many women remain in an abusive relationship.[139] However, domestic violence often becomes so severe that women eventually leave their homes, even when they have no place to go.[140]

Most women who are victims of domestic violence are not aware that there is separate social service funding available to help them, in addition to homelessness services. Free or low-cost legal help is also available to assist with restraining orders and child custody issues. Domestic violence programs can often provide housing or other shelter so you don't have to live in your car as a result of abuse.[141]

Getting Help

You don't have to fight the battle alone. The top "go-to" pages for resources available to you at the national, state, and local level are:

1. The National Domestic Violence Hotline. (http://www.thehotline.org or phone 1-800-799-SAFE (7233). Hotline advocates are available for victims, and anyone calling on their behalf, to provide crisis intervention, safety planning, information, and referrals to agencies in all 50 states, Puerto Rico, and the U.S. Virgin Islands. Assistance is available in English and Spanish, with access to more than 170 languages through interpreter services.

2. The National Coalition Against Domestic Violence. This group provides a master list of national organizations that can help. You can find the list on their website at http://www.ncadv.org/resources/OtherUSOrganizations.php. They also have a state-by-state list of agencies in your area at http://www.ncadv.org/resources/StateCoalitionList.php. Click on your state to find help.

3. The National Network to End Domestic Violence also has a list of national coalitions. You can find them on their website at http://www.nnedv.org/resources/coalitions.html

4. WomensLaw.org is an organization that offers help finding shelters, free or low-cost legal services and representation, and help working with court and law enforcement agencies. The information is state-specific, and written in plain language so that people can comprehend it without the help of a lawyer. The website also provides tips for working with lawyers, and listings for telephone hotlines, local and state programs, court forms, and law enforcement. Visit http://www.womenslaw.org/gethelp.php to find national, state and local services and referrals in your area.

For a list of what to expect from programs, shelters and legal advocates, visit http://www.wscadv.org/getHelpNow.cfm. Services available at the local level can include: Crisis intervention, safety planning, in-person response for survivors of sexual violence, emergency housing resources, "Danger to Safety" transportation assistance, support groups, and referrals to other resources.[142] Some programs are language-based (e.g., Russian, Southeast Asian). There are also school-based prevention programs, support groups and home visits for families leaving domestic violence situations.

Youth

Causes of homelessness among youth fall into three inter-related categories: family problems, economic problems, and residential instability (i.e., aging out of foster care).[143] At least 1.7 million youth run away from home each year, leaving after years of physical and sexual abuse, strained relationships, addiction of a family member, and parental neglect.[144] Other youths may become homeless when their families suffer financial crises resulting from lack of affordable housing, limited employment opportunities, insufficient wages, no medical insurance, or inadequate welfare benefits. These kids become homeless with their families, but are later separated from them by shelter, transitional housing, or child welfare policies.[145]

The same factors that contribute to adult homelessness can lead to youth homelessness: poverty, lack of affordable housing, low education levels, unemployment, mental health issues, and substance abuse.[146] Moreover, the existing homeless assistance system is largely designed for adults. Local nonprofit organizations, shelters, housing projects, and other assistance providers often do not understand the needs of homeless youth, and may lack the resources to provide the necessary interventions.[147]

Homeless youth face difficulties attending school because of legal guardianship requirements, residency requirements, improper records, and lack of transportation. As a result, they face severe challenges in obtaining an education and supporting themselves emotionally and financially.[148]

Because of their age, homeless youth have few legal means by which they can earn enough money to meet basic needs. Many homeless adolescents find that exchanging sex for food, clothing, and shelter is their only chance of survival on the streets.[149]

Homeless adolescents often suffer from severe anxiety and depression, poor health and nutrition, and low self-esteem. In one study, the rates of major depression, conduct disorder, and post-traumatic stress syndrome were found to be three times as high among runaway youth, than youth who have not run away.[150]

National reports have consistently noted the prevalence of lesbian, gay, bisexual, transgender and questioning (LGBTQ) youth in the homeless population. Many experience abandonment and severe family conflict stemming from their sexual orientation and gender identity, but other factors are also present: physical abuse, sexual abuse, neglect, substance abuse by parents, and mental health disabilities. Once homeless, LGBTQ youth experience higher rates of physical and sexual assault, and higher incidence of mental health problems and unsafe sexual behaviors, than heterosexual homeless youth. LGBTQ homeless youth are twice as likely to attempt suicide (62 percent) as their heterosexual homeless peers (29 percent).[151]

Getting Help

Contact the National Runaway Switchboard (NRS) hotline at 1-800-RUNAWAY, or visit their website at http://www.1800runaway.org.[152] Through the hotline and online services, NRS provides crisis intervention, referrals to local resources, and education and prevention services to youth, families and community members throughout the country 24 hours a day, 365 days a year.

The NRS site also has an online bulletin board where teens can ask questions anonymously and share their thoughts and experiences. They can also reach out for help via email at info@1800Runaway.org. There is also a live chat service which allows youth and teens in crisis to access an

NRS crisis intervention specialist, and connect to resources such as shelter, counseling, food, medical and legal assistance.[153]

Via NRS' Home Free program (in partnership with Greyhound Lines, Inc.), runaways and homeless youth can reunite with their families, or an alternative living situation with extended families, through a free bus ticket home.   Over 14,000 youth have been reunited with families through the program since 1995.   NRS can also facilitate conference calls when youth request assistance in contacting their family, or an agency that can help them.   NRS also maintains a message service for youth who want to relay a message but are not ready to communicate directly with their parents.[154]

For educational resources, contact the National Center for Homeless Education (NCHE):

Toll-free helpline:	1-800-308-2145
Helpline email:	homeless@serve.org
Staff general number:	1-800-755-3277
Mailing address:	NCHE at SERVE
	P.O. Box 5367
	Greensboro, NC 27435

Visit the United Way website (http://apps.unitedway.org/myuw) and select your state to find local resources, or call United Way's helpline by dialing 2-1-1 or visiting http://www.211.org.[155]

The Ali Forney Center (AFC) is the nation's largest and most comprehensive organization dedicated to homeless LGBTQ youth. They provide homeless LGBTQ youths (aged 16-24) with support and services to escape the streets, and begin to live healthy and independent lives. Visit their website at http://www.aliforneycenter.org and click on "Get Help."

Veterans

Veterans are at especially high risk for homelessness—about 40% of homeless men are veterans, although veterans comprise only 34 percent of the general adult male population.[156]   A number of factors contribute to homelessness among veterans, including lack of income, physical health and disability, mental health and trauma, substance abuse, and weak social networks.   But it is the lack of affordable housing that is the primary culprit.[157] While most of the 23.4 million U.S. veterans do not have trouble affording housing costs, the analysis found that nearly half a million veterans are extremely low-income, and therefore severely rent burdened (paying more than 50% of their income toward rent). These are the veterans who often become homeless.[158]

Getting Help

The Veterans Administration page at http://va.gov/homeless is the "go to" website for homeless veterans, and the best starting point to find federal benefits that are available.

- The National Call Center for Homeless Veterans 1-877-4AID-VET (or 1-877-424-3838) is a hotline for homeless and at-risk veterans to access VA Services 24/7.

If you don't have access to the Internet, call the phone number above to access the following services available to homeless veterans, as well as veterans at risk of homelessness, and their families: Safe housing, opportunities to return to employment, health care, and mental health services. You can also call 1-800-827-1000 to see what non-homeless veterans benefits are available. For health care needs, call 1-877-222-VETS (8387).

The Veterans Crisis Line connects veterans in crisis (and their families and friends) with Department of Veterans Affairs responders through a confidential, toll-free hotline, online chat, or text:

- Reach the Veterans Crisis Line (suicide prevention) at 1-800-273-TALK (8255) and press 1
- The web site to access the same crisis line service in online chat format instead is http://veteranscrisisline.net
- Text 838255

When you call the hotline, join the online chat, or text:

- You will be connected to a trained VA responder.
- The responder will ask a few questions to assess your needs.
- If you're a veteran, you may be connected with the Homeless Program point of contact at the nearest VA facility.
- Contact information will be requested so staff may follow up.

The hotline and online chat are free (texting fees may apply depending on your particular phone contract), and neither VA registration nor enrollment in VA healthcare is required to use either service. Responders will work with you to help you get through any personal crisis, even if that crisis does not involve thoughts of suicide.[159]

- https://www.nrd.gov/homeless_assistance

The National Resource Directory (NRD) is a website that connects service members, veterans, their families, and caregivers to programs and services that support them at the national, state, and local levels, including support recovery, rehabilitation and community reintegration. You can find information on a variety of topics, such as:

- Benefits & Compensation
- Education & Training
- Employment
- Family & Caregiver Support
- Health
- Homeless Assistance
- Housing

- • Transportation & Travel
- • Volunteer Opportunities
- • Other Services & Resources

- • http://www.hudhre.info/VeteransAssistance

For housing, the HUD Homelessness Resource Exchange Veteran's Assistance site is a one-stop spot for veterans, and those who help veterans, to find housing. On this page are HUD homeless veteran programs and initiatives, as well as resources, publications, and relevant links to agencies and organizations. Additionally, to make the programs more easily accessible, there is local contact information for each program.[160]

- • http://www.va.gov/HOMELESS/docs/HCHV_Sites_ByState.pdf

Find homeless veterans health care contacts by state.

- • http://www.justiceforvets.org/veterans-treatment-court-locations

The above site lists veterans treatment court programs and locations.

- • http://nchv.org/index.php/help/help/step-by-step

The National Coalition for Homeless Veterans pages list help that is immediately available, and step-by-step guides to help you figure out which services you might need.

- • http://www.ruralhealth.va.gov

To better serve veterans in rural areas, VA's Office of Rural Health (ORH) was established in 2007 to improve access and quality of health care for rural veterans and Native American veterans in tribal communities. Veterans living in rural areas have traditionally been underserved for health care access.

- https://www.nrd.gov/jobSearch/index

The Veterans Job Bank provides a central resource that allows veterans to access jobs available specifically for them.

Rural

Rural homelessness, like urban homelessness, is the result of poverty and a lack of affordable housing. In 2005, research showed that the odds of being poor are between 1.2 to 2.3 times higher for people in non-metropolitan areas, than in metropolitan areas. Rural residential histories reveal that homelessness is often precipitated by a structural or physical housing problem jeopardizing health or safety; when families relocate to safer housing, the rent is often too much to manage and they experience homelessness again while searching for housing that is both safe and affordable. While housing costs are lower in rural areas, so are rural incomes, leading to similarly high rent burdens.[161] Other trends affecting rural homelessness include the distance between low-cost housing and employment opportunities, lack of transportation, decline in home ownership, restrictive land-use regulations and housing codes, rising rent burdens, and insecure tenancy resulting from changes in the local real estate market (i.e., the displacement of trailer park residents).[162] Longer periods of unemployment also plague the rural poor more often than their urban counterparts.[163]

Rural homelessness is most pronounced in rural regions that are primarily agricultural; regions whose economies are based on declining extractive industries such as mining, timber, or fishing; and regions experiencing economic growth. This occurs because areas with industrial plants attract more workers than jobs available, and areas near urban centers attract new businesses and higher-income residents, which drive up taxes and living expenses.

Rural homelessness is a double-edged sword, because there is less transitional housing, fewer employment programs, fewer social service agencies, and fewer health care programs than in cities. However, finding solutions for homeless people can be easier in rural areas, in part because the numbers aren't so overwhelming. "Take the extreme, say Los Angeles, that has a city's worth of homeless people, 60,000 or 70,000 homeless people. It's difficult to think what you might do about that," says Nan Roman, president of the National Alliance to End Homelessness. "Whereas rural communities...may have 10 or 12 homeless people."[164]

Also, understanding rural homelessness requires a more flexible definition of homelessness. There are far fewer shelters in rural areas than in urban areas, so people experiencing homelessness are less likely to live on the street or in a shelter. Instead, they are more likely to live in a car or camper, or with relatives, in overcrowded or substandard housing. Restricting definitions of homelessness to include only those who are literally homeless —that is, on the streets or in shelters—does not fit well with the rural reality, and also may exclude many rural communities from accessing federal dollars to address homelessness.[165]

About 9% of all homeless people live in rural areas. Studies comparing urban and rural homeless populations have shown that homeless people in rural areas are more likely to be white, female, married, currently working, homeless for the first time, and homeless for a shorter period of time. Other research indicates that families, single mothers, and children make up the largest group of people who are homeless in rural areas.[166]

Rural areas have fewer service providers, and the rural homeless may have to travel long distances to find them. The service providers that do exist in rural communities differ from their urban counterparts in that they tend to provide less shelter and housing than outreach, food, and financial assistance.[167]

Getting Help

- http://www.raconline.org

The Rural Assistance Center (RAC) is the best online starting point to find programs specifically addressing rural homelessness.

- http://ric.nal.usda.gov/rural-housing-0

The U.S. Department of Agriculture Rural Information Center (RIC) website provides information on housing programs and services for rural areas.

- http://www.rurdev.usda.gov/HSF_SFH.html
- http://www.rurdev.usda.gov/LP_Subject_HousingAndCommunity Assistance.html

The USDA Rural Development page provides information on Housing and Community Facilities Programs (HCFP) in rural areas. The Single Family Housing Programs website (http://www.rurdev.usda.gov/HSF_SFH.html) provides information about home ownership opportunities for low- and moderate-income rural Americans through several loan, grant, and loan guarantee programs. The programs also make funding available to individuals for financing vital improvements necessary to make their homes decent, safe, and sanitary. If you find a program that suits your needs, contact your state USDA service center for help applying to the program at http://offices.sc.egov.usda.gov/locator/app.

Chronic

For many, homelessness is a short-term problem. For others, homelessness is pervasive. According to HUD's definition, a person who is "chronically homeless" is an unaccompanied homeless individual with a disabling condition (i.e., substance abuse, serious mental illness, developmental disability, or chronic physical illness) who has either been continuously homeless for a year or more, or has had at least four episodes of homelessness in the past three years (with homelessness defined as sleeping in a place not meant for human habitation and/or in an emergency homeless shelter).[168]

Twenty three percent of homeless people are reported as chronically homeless.[169] Although they represent a small portion of the overall homeless population, they consume over half of services.[170] Health care is the biggest expense associated with the use of public services by the chronically homelessness, due to frequent and avoidable emergency room visits, inpatient hospitalizations, sobering centers, and nursing homes.[171] The mortality rate for those experiencing chronic homelessness is four to nine times higher than for the general population.

The chronically homelessness also have high rates of incarceration, often for offenses that are non-violent and related to mental illness, or the realities of living on the street. This adds an additional burden to a justice system already stretched to its limit.[172]

Providing permanent supportive housing for people experiencing chronic homelessness is highly cost-effective. Permanent supportive housing leads to dramatic drops in utilization rates for hospitals, ERs, and other major services, as well as drops in arrest rates.[173] The cost of the housing subsidy and supportive services is more than offset by less frequent use of costly public services, such as jails and emergency rooms.[174]

Getting Help

•   http://homelessness.samhsa.gov

The Substance Abuse and Mental Health Services Administration (SAMHSA) homelessness resource center website includes a suicide prevention hotline 1-800-273-TALK (8255); and a treatment locator and referral line 1-800-662-HELP (4357). Additional information is also available at the main Substance Abuse and Mental Health Services Administration (SAMHSA) website at http://www.samhsa.gov.

To search for free or low-cost addiction treatment centers, visit http://www.freeaddictioncenters.com.

For treatment centers that are free, affordable, discounted, low-cost, sliding scale or Medicaid-based, call 1-800-780-2294 to speak with a drug or alcohol counselor, or visit http://www.freetreatmentcenters.com and search by state.

APPENDIX C - CHECKLISTS & KITS

Thrift stores carry clothing, suitcases, and backpacks for far less than you'd pay at discount stores. In some places, Goodwill has outlet stores where you can buy clothing and other textiles by weight. Many winter items, such as high-end, brand name fleece and down, can be purchased at the outlet stores for less than $3 apiece. So dollar stores, thrift stores and outlet thrift stores will save you a fortune.

One gallon-sized, plastic zip-top bags are your best friend. *All* liquids, such as shampoos and soap, should be sealed in them to keep from spilling or leaking over the bottom of your suitcase and everything else, including your car.

Below is a list of items you'll need. Do *not* feel overwhelmed—tackle acquiring and assembling everything a little bit at a time, especially if you have a few weeks until you have to live out of your car.

BEDDING

- Pillow
- Blanket(s) (Lightweight in summer, down for winter)
- Padding, such as a sleeping bag, to lay on as a cushion, and to protect from "chassis chill" for SUVs, pickup trucks with a canopy, or stationwagons
- Lightweight sheet or blanket to cover yourself from view while sleeping

- For SUVs, stationwagons and pickup trucks, a plastic tarp or drop cloth to place under your bedding to prevent condensation and dirt from getting on your bedding.

FOOD

- Juice for quick energy when you get low blood sugar from stress. Child-sized, multi-pack juice boxes with straws are economical (dollar stores carry them), convenient, and space-saving.
- Some small plastic bags of bulk food (rice, beans, etc.) if you have, or can find access to a camp stove
- Manual can opener with bottle opener. Check thrift stores first for these. They cost around $5 new at the grocery store.
- Plastic bag containing plastic knives, forks, spoons and drinking straws
- At least two gallons (or more) of water

HYGIENE BAG

- Should contain all of the kits listed in the next section [See: Kits]
- Deodorant
- Liquid soap or body wash in trial-size bottles (refill them from large bottles kept in the car or storage unit)
- TP - Buying four-packs isn't economical, but they also won't take up as much space as a 16-roll pack
- Paper towels - Again, individual or three-packs aren't as economical as larger sizes, but won't take up a lot of space
- Laundry soap (too expensive to buy in laundromats; can find on sale in dollar stores)
- Women: pads/tampons; makeup for job interviews
- Hairbrush or comb, and hair dryer (and style irons for women)
- Toothbrush, toothpaste and floss. (Not travel-size, as they are more as expensive than regular-size, and won't last as long.)
- Men: shaving kit (See: Kits, below)

CLOTHING BAGS/BOXES

How much of each type you can store will depend on the size of your vehicle. Roll your clothing, rather than folding it, to keep items wrinkle-free and compact, which will allow for more room in a bag or suitcase.

- Casual (jeans, t-shirts)
- Work (dresses, skirts, slacks)
- Socks
- Underwear

SHOES

Winter: Snow boots; waterproof mocs, chukkas, or muck shoes; work shoes, sneakers, shower flip flops
Summer: Work shoes, sandals, tennis shoes

MISCELLANEOUS

- Small bottle of liquid dish soap (re-use plastic utensils by washing them in a plastic zip bag with a little dish soap). You can also reuse a half-gallon, plastic milk container by putting some dish soap in it, and filling it with water to have pre-made, ready-to-use cleanser for hands, utensils, etc.
- Cell phone with charger. Use Google Voice if you don't want the expense of a cell phone.
- Flashlight - Keep a large, heavy-duty flashlight (such as a Maglight) for use outside the vehicle at night, and a small LED flashlight (which uses disc-like watch batteries that can easily be bought in five-packs at a dollar store) for inside the car. Wrap your hand around the lens to focus the light to a small area so a lot of needless flickering and flashing doesn't attract attention from passerby.
- Envelopes with stamps pre-attached
- Sewing kit and several large safety pins
- Butane lighter - Often used to start barbecue grills, this long, slender device is about the same price, and far more waterproof than matches. You can get them at a dollar store.

- Antibacterial wipes - To clean up with after dumping cat litter, using the bathroom, spills, etc.
- Baby wipes
- Small (quart) bottle of bleach - You'll mostly use this for laundry, but you can also disinfect water with it, too.
- Notebook (or notepad) and pens - You'd be surprised how much you need these to leave messages, write down phone numbers, or make lists.
- Duct tape - Will hold up Reflectix or other window shades.
- Box of gallon freezer zip plastic bags, or plastic produce bag end roll from bulk food section (ask a produce clerk).
- Box of kitchen-sized garbage bags
- Box of black leaf or garbage bags (can use for laundry bags)

CAR MAINTENANCE

These items should always be in your car whether you are living in it or not:

- Oil
- Rags (can also use paper towels)
- Jumper cables (optional)
- Extra taillight bulbs
- Unmarked spare car key - This can be buried in a plastic bag under a bush in a park (or other location if you are staying in one vicinity). Otherwise, keep it in your storage unit, or with a friend.
- Spare car key on your physical person (either in your wallet or taped to the back of your cell phone) at all times.
- Screwdrivers, pliers and hammer
- Antifreeze
- De-icer gallon (winter)
- Ice scraper (winter)

KITS

Each kit should be contained within one or two gallon-sized, plastic zip-top bags. Most of these items can be purchased at a dollar store, if you don't already have them on hand.

Toothbrush Kit

- New toothbrush
- Toothbrush travel case; make sure it has holes for ventilation
- Toothpaste
- Floss
- Washcloth or hand towel
- Empty plastic cup for rinse water (small, clean, yogurt containers are great for this)

Shower Kit

- Mini, refillable bottles of shampoo and conditioner
- Mini, refillable bottles of liquid body wash soap. Bars of soap take too long to dry out after use.
- Mini, refillable bottles of lotion or skin moisturizer; can be bought as needed in bulk
- Razors (disposable, multi-pack)
- Bath towel and two hand towels (one for hair, one for hands); all rolled to save space
- Agave washcloth or terry washcloths (the mesh-like agave dries faster)
- Deodorant - Don't buy extra; it's already in the hygiene bag above—just remember to bring it with you when you shower
- Flip flops (a must, especially if using dirty shower facilities)
- Hairdryer, style iron, and styling products; already in the hygiene bag above—just remember to bring it with you when you shower

Men's Shaving Kit

- Washcloth or hand towel
- Shaving lotion and aftershave
- Razors (disposable, multi-pack)

- Empty plastic cup to hold razor rinse water (small, clean yogurt containers are great for this)

Medical Kit (Medicines & First Aid Supplies)

- Medications. Switching to generic drugs can help, because most large discount merchants and grocery stores offer 90-day supplies for around $10. You can also keep just a few pills you rarely use (such as anti-diarrhea medicine) in a plastic pill container, and put the rest of the box or bottle in storage.
- Vitamins.
- Rubbing Alcohol - A better topical antiseptic than hydrogen peroxide, and due to high flammability, can double as a fire igniter if needed.
- Hydrogen Peroxide - A topical antiseptic for minor cuts and scrapes (but not as effective at killing bacteria as rubbing alcohol), and stain remover. It also removes ear wax when diluted 50-50 with water (use warm water or it will create dizziness).
- Plastic or fabric adhesive bandages
- Tweezers - Great for removing splinters or burrs
- Scissors - To either open packages or cut duct tape
- Pain reliever - Some people prefer aspirin; others prefer acetaminophen or ibuprofen. Generics are available in dollar stores.
- Charcoal pills - Really, no kidding, if you get food poisoning, this stuff will knock it out quickly.
- Latex gloves - Helpful for many things, including really nasty messes (e.g., scrubbing cat vomit off a blanket by hand when the water pressure from a hose isn't enough.)

APPENDIX D - WEBSITES & ORGANIZATIONS

- http://americawhatwentwrong.org/story/How-banks-government-fail
- http://americawhatwentwrong.org/stories/excerpt-the-betrayal-of-the-american-dream
- http://americawhatwentwrong.org/story/restoring-american-dream

Donald L. Barlett and James B. Steele are one of the most widely acclaimed investigative reporting teams in American journalism. They have won two Pulitzer Prizes for their bestselling *America: What Went Wrong?* series, which outlines how the country got itself into its plutocracy, and how it can get out. Loaded with facts, and yet easy to read and understand, this book is the ultimate source in understanding the country's current—and future—problems.

- http://www.ihatemylife.us/homeless.html
- http://www.ihatemylife.us/help.html

Don't let the name of the website fool you—this is one of the most stunningly well-researched, thoughtful, comprehensive, and well-written car living websites in existence. It addresses every major problem facing car dwellers, and has tons of practical information and resources to combat them. Like this book, it's about helping you through and getting you out of homelessness via every imaginable resource possible.

- http://www.nationalhomeless.org/want_to_help/index.html

A list you can point others to if they want to help end homelessness.

- http://www.amazon.com/Dwelling-Portably-1980-89-Bert-Davis/dp/1934620084

Bert and Holly Davis' *Dwelling Portably* series is a great resource. They have lived for years in a forest in rural Oregon, and have multiple, do-it-yourself solutions and informative tips for showering, cooking, and living far outside of cities without technology. I subscribed to their newsletter years ago; it's nice to see all of them compiled into books now.

- http://www.nasna.org/members-and-services

Street newspapers play a vital role in building self-confidence and self-worth among the homeless. The North American Street Newspaper Association (NASNA) represents 31 street newspapers that work with more than 1,500 individuals experiencing homelessness and poverty, and who gain immediate income through the sales of the newspaper every month. NASNA is a growing grassroots media network with a circulation of 300,000.

- http://realchangenews.org/index.php/site/about/org

Real Change publishes the only "street newspaper" in Washington State, and the only newspaper that consistently focuses on poverty, homelessness, and social justice. Real Change provides opportunity and a voice for low-income and homeless people, while taking action for economic justice.

- http://www.survivethestreets.org

Survive the Streets is a giveaway event aimed at serving people who sleep outside with the gear they need to survive the winter. Their model can easily be duplicated in other cities.

- http://www.wikihow.com/Live-in-Your-Car
- http://www.quora.com/Sleep/How-can-I-most-inconspicuously-sleep-in-my-car
- http://survivingthemiddleclasscrash.wordpress.com/2012/03/04/how-to-live-in-your-car
- http://guide2homelessness.blogspot.com

Most of the car living ideas from the above websites are covered in this book, but they give another perspective.

- http://showertothepeople.org
- http://www.facebook.com/pages/Shower-to-the-People-Inc/399443756749869

Shower to the People is a Portland, Oregon-based nonprofit which provides free basic hygiene to house-less individuals (or anyone else without access to hygiene), by taking a shower trailer with two complete bathrooms to people where they live, on the street. This essential program has also been replicated in other cities—check to see if there is a similar one in your area.[175]

NATIONAL ORGANIZATIONS (in alphabetical order)

- AARDVARC: An Abuse, Rape & Domestic Violence Aid & Resource Collection (http://www.aardvarc.org)
- Alone Without A Home: A State-By-State Review of Laws Affecting Unaccompanied Youth (Sept. 2012) - (http://www.nlchp.org/content/pubs/Alone%20Without%20a %20Home,%20FINAL1.pdf)
- Center on Adolescent Health and the Law (http://www.cahl.org)
- Children Exposed to Domestic Violence: A Teacher's Handbook to Increase Understanding and Improve Community Responses (2002), by Linda L. Baker et al., available at (http://www.lfcc.on.ca/teacher-us.PDF)
- Corporation for Supportive Housing (http://www.csh.org)
- Family Violence Prevention Fund (http://endabuse.org)
- Homeless Shelter Directory (http://www.homelessshelterdirectory.org) and (http://www.shelterlistings.org/find_shelter.html)
- Housing Assistance Council Rural Homelessness (http://homeless.samhsa.gov/resourcefiles/neqkwasx.pdf)
- HUD Homelessness Resource Exchange (http://www.hudhre.info/index.cfm? do=viewHomelessResources)
- Institute for Children, Poverty, and Homelessness (http://www.icphusa.org)
- National Alliance to End Homelessness (http://www.endhomelessness.org)
- National Association for the Education of Homeless Children and Youth (http://www.naehcy.org)
- National Center for Homeless Education (http://www.serve.org/nche)
- National Center on Family Homelessness (http://www.familyhomelessness.org)

- National Clearinghouse on Families and Youth (http://ncfy.acf.hhs.gov)
- National Coalition Against Domestic Violence (http://www.ncadv.org)
- National Coalition for the Homeless (http://www.nationalhomeless.org)
- National Domestic Violence Hotline (http://www.ndvh.org) 1-800-799-SAFE (7233) or (TTY) 1-800-787-3224
- National Health Care for the Homeless Council (http://www.nhchc.org)
- National Law Center on Homelessness & Poverty (http://www.nlchp.org)
- National Low Income Housing Coalition (http://nlihc.org)
- National Network for Youth (http://www.nn4youth.org)
- National Network to End Domestic Violence (http://www.nnedv.org)
- National Policy and Advocacy Council on Homelessness (http://www.npach.org)
- National Sexual Assault Hotline - 1-800-656-HOPE
- Public Housing Network (http://www.publichousing.com)
- Stalking Resource Center - 1-800-FYI-CALL, M-F 8:30 a.m.-8:30 p.m. EST, or email: gethelp@ncvc.org
- U.S. Department of Education, Education for Homeless Children and Youth Program (http://www.ed.gov/programs/homeless/index.html)
- US Interagency Council on Homelessness (http://www.usich.gov)
- Women's Law. org (http://womenslaw.org) - Provides legal information and support to victims of domestic violence and sexual assault
- Women's Law.org Email Legal Hotline (http://hotline.womenslaw.org)

ENDNOTES

Introduction

1   https://www.onecpd.info/resources/documents/RuralCoCGuidebook.pdf

2   http://www.smh.com.au/nsw/tourist-attacked-while-sleeping-in-car-20121130-2alh6.html and http://www.smh.com.au/nsw/woman-sleeping-in-car-attacked-by-man-police-20121001-26uop.html and http://www.mercedsunstar.com/2012/08/28/2502462/sleeping-traveler-attacked-by.html

3   http://www.guardian.co.uk/commentisfree/belief/2013/jan/25/austerity-squeezed-middle-homeless-suffering?CMP=twt_gu

Section 1 - Who Are The Car-Dwelling Homeless?

4   http://seattletimes.com/html/localnews/2016849799_carcamping25m.html

5   http://www.ehow.com/about_4574563_dont-homeless-people-stay-shelters.html

6   http://www.destination-home.info/Homelessness/Data/national.htm

7   http://www.nlchp.org/hapia.cfm

8   http://usatoday30.usatoday.com/news/nation/2009-05-04-new-homeless_N.htm

9   http://www.time.com/time/nation/article/0,8599,1956213,00.html

10   "With Shelters Full, Homeless Family Sent to Woods Instead." WPSD Local 6 TV. Paducah, KY. http://www.wpsdlocal6.com/news/local/No-room-for-families-at-shelters-sent-to-woods-instead-119448789.html

11   http://www.cbsnews.com/video/watch/?id=7389750n. Scott Pelley of 60 Minutes: "Hard Times Generation: Families living in cars."

Section 2 - What To Do Before Living In Your Car

12   http://www.goodwillnmi.org/goodwillinn/?fuseaction=article&articleid=739

13   http://www.ihatemylife.us/story.html

14   http://www.goodwillnmi.org/homeless-housing/goodwill-inn-homeless-shelter/homeless-need-help/

15   http://www.endhomelessness.org/pages/faqs#help

16   http://www.fema.gov/pdf/areyouready/appendix_b.pdf . See also: http://www.seattle.gov/emergency/library/publiceducation/supplieskit/Your%20Family%20Disaster%20Supplies%20Kit.pdf and http://www.ready.gov/sites/default/files/documents/files/checklist_1.pdf

Section 3 - Car Living Basics

17   http://www.dailynews.com/news/ci_20007036

18   http://www.ihatemylife.us/story.html

19   http://www.wikihow.com/Live-in-Your-Car

20   http://www.cars.com/go/advice/Story.jsp?section=ins&subject=ins_req&story=state-insurance-requirements

21   To find your car's square footage, go to http://www.endmemo.com/cconvert/ft3ft2.php

Section 4 - During Car Living: Situations & Scenarios

22   http://www.ihatemylife.us/homeless.html

23   http://homebuying.about.com/cs/saferooms/a/disaster_kit.htm

24   http://www.blm.gov/or/resources/recreation/files/brochures/portabletoilets.pdf

25   http://www.doc.govt.nz/parks-and-recreation/plan-and-prepare/care-codes/activity-minimal-impact-codes/disposing-of-human-waste/

26   http://www.nlchp.org/hapia.cfm and
http://www.nationalhomeless.org/factsheets/families.html

27   http://www.nlchp.org/content/pubs/Some%20Facts%20on%20Homeless%20and%20DV.pdf

28   http://www.familyhomelessness.org/families.php?p=ts

29   http://www.housethehomeless.org/children-experiencing-homelessness/

30   http://wraphome.org/downloads/2010%20Update%20Without%20Housing.pdf

31   http://center.serve.org/nche/downloads/briefs/domestic.pdf

32   http://center.serve.org/nche/downloads/briefs/domestic.pdf

33   http://center.serve.org/nche/downloads/briefs/domestic.pdf

34   http://www.in.gov/fssa/dfr/2684.htm

35   http://www.familyhomelessness.org/media/306.pdf. Citations and source material include:

- Culhane, JF et al. (2003). Prevalence of child welfare services involvement among homeless and low-income mothers: A five-year birth cohort study. Journal of Sociology and Social Welfare. 30(3)
- US Conference of Mayors. (2006). Hunger and Homelessness Survey. Available at www.usmayors.org.
- National Center on Family Homelessness, 1999.
- Bassuk, EL et al, 1996.
- Zlotnick, C. et al. (1998). Foster care children and family homelessness. American Journal of Public Health. 88(9): 1368-1370;
- Roman, N. et al. (1995). Web of Failure: The Relationship between Foster Care and Homelessness. Washington, DC: National Alliance to End Homelessness. Available at www.endhomelessness.org.
- National Center on Family Homelessness, 1999; Pettit, MR et al (1997). *Child Abuse and Neglect: A look at the States.* Washington DC: Child Welfare League of America Press, pp 72-75.
- Doerre, Y.A. et al. (1996). *Home Sweet Home.* Washington, DC: Children's Welfare League of America Press.

36   http://www.hhs.gov/homeless/research/endhomelessness.html

37   http://money.howstuffworks.com/homeless4.htm

38   http://www.nctsnet.org/nctsn_assets/pdfs/promising_practices/Facts_on_Trauma_and_Homeless_Children.pdf

39   http://olympiawa.gov/community/parks/parks-and-trails/heritage-park-fountain

40   http://www.hobopoet.com/car-living-skills/ (in the comments section)

41   http://www.survivethestreets.org

42   http://www.amazon.com/Heated-Fleece-Travel-Electric-Blanket/product-reviews/B000V8QVX6/ref=cm_cr_dp_qt_hist_five?
      ie=UTF8&filterBy=addFiveStar&showViewpoints=0.

      See also: Wagan IN9738-5 12-Volt Heated Seat Cushion (on sale $14.95 from Amazon);
      the Heated Fleece Travel Electric Blanket - 12 Volt - Red Plaid-($26 from Amazon); and a
      Roadpro 12V, 2 Outlet Platinum Series Fused Cigarette Lighter Adapter with Short
      Cord ($8.50 from Amazon).

43   The way this heater works is when propane is brought into contact with oxygen in the
      air in the presence of a catalyst, the resulting chemical reaction generates heat. See:
      http://www.mrheater.com/faq.aspx?id=22

44   https://www.safelinkwireless.com/Enrollment/Safelink/en/Public/NewHome.html

45   Visit their website https://www.usps.com/manage/get-a-po-box.htm

46   http://about.usps.com/forms/ps1093.pdf

47   https://www.usps.com/manage/get-a-po-box.htm

48   http://www.wikihow.com/Rent-a-Post-Office-Box

49   http://about.usps.com/forms/ps1093.pdf

50   http://about.usps.com/forms/ps1093.pdf

51   http://faq.usps.com/eCustomer/iq/usps/request.do?create=kb:USPSFAQ. Search for
      "Hold for pickup service."

52   https://www.usps.com/manage/forward-mail.htm

53   http://www.nydailynews.com/news/homeless-mail-general-delivery-article-1.276023

54   http://www.wikihow.com/Live-in-Your-Car

55   http://www.motivemag.com/pub/feature/drivers_ed/Motive_Culture_How_to_Live_In_
      Your_Car.shtml

56   http://www.ihatemylife.us/story.html

57   http://www.smh.com.au/nsw/woman-sleeping-in-car-attacked-by-man-police-
      20121001-26uop.html

58   http://www.nytimes.com/2006/04/02/us/02cars.html?pagewanted=all&_r=0

59   http://corporate.walmart.com/frequently-asked-questions#Park_RV

60   http://www.walmartcrimereport.com/ and
      http://ufcw770.org/sites/all/themes/danland/files/CrimeAndWalmart.pdf

61   http://www.jrrobertssecurity.com/articles/wal-mart-parking-lot-crime.htm and
      http://www.walmartmovie.com/

62   http://www.homelessshelterdirectory.org/cgi-bin/id/article.cgi?article=20. "The New
      Homeless" by Alexandra Pauley. See also:
      https://www.facebook.com/QuantumReaction

63   http://money.howstuffworks.com/homeless5.htm

64   http://blogs.smithsonianmag.com/science/2011/11/the-myth-of-the-frozen-jeans/

65   http://www.nctsnet.org/nctsn_assets/pdfs/promising_practices/Facts_on_Trauma_and_
      Homeless_Children.pdf

66   http://www.salon.com/2013/03/07/public_libraries_the_new_homeless_shelters_partner

67   http://www.newstatesman.com/voices/2013/01/people-without-homes-not-homeless-
      people (Username backwards7 from comments section)

68   http://www.crisis.org.uk/pages/relationship-breakdown-and-lonliness.html

69   http://www.ihatemylife.us/story.html

70   http://www.ihatemylife.us/story.html

71   http://blogs.scientificamerican.com/observations/2011/11/16/can-extreme-resilience-be-taught/ and http://www.examiner.com/article/us-navy-seal-experts-give-us-olympic-contenders-a-competitive-edge

72   http://blog.smu.edu/research/2010/12/16/a-new-breathing-therapy-reduces-panic-and-anxiety-by-reversing-hyperventilation/ and http://www.plosone.org/article/info%3Adoi%2F10.1371%2Fjournal.pone.0046597 and http://www.psmag.com/health/performance-anxiety-take-a-deep-breath-47882/

      The main article I am referring to in the text is from:
      http://olympics.time.com/2012/07/02/trained-by-seals/

73   http://realchangenews.org/

74   http://vetmedicine.about.com/gi/o.htm?
      zi=1/XJ&zTi=1&sdn=vetmedicine&cdn=homegarden&tm=10&f=00&tt=50&bt=0&bts=0
      &zu=http%3A//www.mydogiscool.com/x_car_study.php   AND
      http://www.newscientist.com/article/dn7631

75   A homeless man in Washington state was saved by his dog:
      http://www.kirotv.com/news/news/homeless-man-rescued-after-attaching-help-note-dog/nWJhd/

76   http://www.nationalhomeless.org/publications/fivefundamentals/Five_Fundamentals_Statement.pdf

77   http://money.howstuffworks.com/homeless4.htm

78   http://www.endhomelessness.org/pages/mental_physical_health

79   http://www.mrsh.net/firststep/firststep%20%28d%29/content/healthcategory.html

80   http://www.investopedia.com/articles/pf/07/medicare-vs-medicaid.asp#ixzz2LZkfJiMh

81   http://www.familyhomelessness.org/assistance.php?p=f

82   In addition to $10/90-day supply generic prescriptions, there are also $4/30-day supply generics available. Some retail chains offer extensive lists of generic drugs at low cost. Here are a few:

      | Giant Eagle | 30-day supply $4 |
      | K-Mart | 30-day supply $4 |
      | Kroger Rx | 30-day supply $4 |
      | Target | 30-day supply $4 |
      | WalMart | 30-day supply $4 |
      | Winn Dixie | 30-day supply $4 |
      | ShopRite | 30-day supply $4 |
      | Fred Myer | 30-day supply $4 |
      | Pathmark | 30-day supply $4 |

83   http://www.mayoclinic.com/health/depression-and-exercise/MH00043

84   http://www.nationalhomeless.org/publications/fivefundamentals/Five_Fundamentals_Statement.pdf

85   http://www.aolnews.com/2010/11/07/smile-your-license-plates-on-towns-candid-camera/ and
      http://www.nationalhomeless.org/publications/crimreport/meanestcities.html

Section 5 - After Homelessness

86   http://www.nytimes.com/2006/04/02/us/02cars.html?pagewanted=all&_r=0 and
      http://www.huduser.org/portal/datasets/fmr.html and
      http://www.endhomelessness.org/pages/faqs#why

87 http://www.nytimes.com/1988/12/19/us/defying-popular-stereotypes-many-of-homeless-have-jobs.html?pagewanted=all&src=pm>

88 http://www.newyorker.com/online/blogs/comment/2013/02/the-case-for-a-higher-minimum-wage.html and
http://www.newyorker.com/online/blogs/johncassidy/2013/02/the-case-for-a-higher-minimum-wage.html?intcid=obnetwork and http://www.ncsl.org/issues-research/labor/state-minimum-wage-chart.aspx

89 http://www.needymeds.org/indices/povertyguidelines.htm

90 http://www.huffingtonpost.com/sanjay-sanghoee/walmart-minimum-wage_b_2223877.html and http://www.huffingtonpost.com/sanjay-sanghoee/minimum-wage_b_2175801.html. See also: http://blogs.wsj.com/economics/2013/03/30/number-of-the-week-college-grads-in-minimum-wage-jobs/

91 http://www.huffingtonpost.com/sanjay-sanghoee/walmart-minimum-wage_b_2223877.html

92 http://www.sciencedaily.com/releases/2012/09/120905141920.htm and
http://business.time.com/2012/01/05/the-loss-of-upward-mobility-in-the-u-s/ and
http://www.economist.com/node/3518560 and
http://www.nytimes.com/2012/01/05/us/harder-for-americans-to-rise-from-lower-rungs.html?hp&_r=0

93 http://money.howstuffworks.com/homeless5.htm

94 http://www.goodwillnmi.org/homeless-housing/goodwill-inn-homeless-shelter/homeless-need-help/

95 http://www.shelterlistings.org/find_shelter.html

96 http://www.nimh.nih.gov/health/publications/post-traumatic-stress-disorder-ptsd/what-are-the-symptoms-of-ptsd.shtml

97 http://www.nimh.nih.gov/health/publications/post-traumatic-stress-disorder-ptsd/what-are-the-symptoms-of-ptsd.shtml

98 http://www.nimh.nih.gov/health/publications/post-traumatic-stress-disorder-ptsd/where-can-i-go-for-help.shtml

Section 6 - Advocating For Change

99   http://www.nlchp.org/hapia.cfm

100 http://www.nlchp.org/hapia.cfm

101 U.S. Conference of Mayors 2011 Status Report on Hunger & Homelessness: http://usmayors.org/pressreleases/uploads/2011-hhreport.pdf

102 http://www.hud.gov/offices/cpd/affordablehousing/

103 http://nlihc.org/oor/2013

104 http://nlihc.org/oor/2013

105 http://nlihc.org/article/housing spotlight-volume-3-issue-1 and
http://www.census.gov/acs/www/

106 http://nlihc.org/sites/default/files/HS_3-1.pdf

107 http://nlihc.org/sites/default/files/HS_3-1.pdf

108 http://homeless.samhsa.gov/channel/Homelessness-Prevention-410.aspx

109 http://www.ocpp.org/media/uploads/pdf/2012/07/fs20120719SWO2Inequality2010update_fnl_.pdf

110 Here is a simple to use federal poverty line calculator:
http://www.needymeds.org/indices/FPL_Calculator.html.

111 http://www.nelp.org/page/-/Job_Creation/LowWageRecovery2012.pdf?nocdn=1

112   http://americawhatwentwrong.org/story/1-in-3-families-now-working-poor/

113   http://www.thirteen.org/metrofocus/2013/03/minimum-wage-debate-heats-up/

114   http://www.people-press.org/files/legacy-pdf/02-21-13%20Political%20Release.pdf and
http://www.thirteen.org/metrofocus/2013/03/minimum-wage-debate-heats-up/

115   http://www.raisetheminimumwage.com/

116   http://livingwage.mit.edu/

117   http://nelp.3cdn.net/e555b2e361f8f734f4_sim6btdzo.pdf

118   http://nelp.3cdn.net/e555b2e361f8f734f4_sim6btdzo.pdf and
http://www.raisetheminimumwage.com/pages/corporate-profits

119   http://www.huffingtonpost.com/2013/03/04/minimum-wage_n_2807440.html and
http://boingboing.net/2012/11/23/how-walmart-uses-medicaid-and.html and
http://www.opensecrets.org/lobby/clientsum.php?id=D000000367&year=2011

120   http://www.ocpp.org/media/uploads/pdf/2013/03/fs20130326TaxesEconomicGrowth_fnl
.pdf

121   http://en.wikipedia.org/wiki/Citizens_United_v._Federal_Election_Commission

122   http://www.time.com/time/nation/article/0,8599,1956213,00.html

123   http://nelp.3cdn.net/02b725e73dc24e0644_0im6bkno9.pdf

124   http://www.forbes.com/sites/jonbruner/2012/02/08/hey-wanna-buy-some-influence/
and http://www.forbes.com/sites/danielfisher/2012/02/08/for-billionaires-politics-is-
the-cheapest-asset-around/

125   http://www.svdp.us/what-we-do/homeless-services/overnight-parking-program/

126   http://seattletimes.com/html/localnews/2020216841_homelessxml.html

127   http://www.time.com/time/nation/article/0,8599,1956213,00.html

128   http://www.endhomelessness.org/library/entry/fact-sheet-what-is-a-ten-year-plan-to-
end-homelessness

129   http://americawhatwentwrong.org/story/How-banks-government-fail/

130   http://americawhatwentwrong.org/story/How-banks-government-fail/

131   http://www.ihatemylife.us/story.html

132   http://americawhatwentwrong.org/story/How-banks-government-fail/

Appendix A - Additional Resources

133   http://www.familyhomelessness.org/assistance.php?p=f

134   http://www.needymeds.org/indices/cantfindmeds.htm

Appendix B - Help for Specific Types of Homelessness

135   http://www.nlchp.org/content/pubs/Some%20Facts%20on%20Homeless%20and
%20DV.pdf

136   http://www.newdestinyhousing.org/what-we-do/facts-a-stats

137   http://www.nnedv.org/docs/Policy/NNEDV_DVHousing__factsheet.pdf

138   National Alliance to End Homelessness:
http://www.endhomelessness.org/pages/domestic_violence

139   http://www.nlchp.org/content/pubs/Some%20Facts%20on%20Homeless%20and
%20DV.pdf

140   http://www.futureswithoutviolence.org/userfiles/file/Children_and_Families/facts_hou
sing_dv.pdf

141   http://www.ojp.usdoj.gov/bjs/intimate/ipv.htm.

Find more Resources:
- Bureau of Justice Statistics, Office of Justice Programs. Intimate Partner Violence in the United States.
- Centers for Disease Control and Prevention, Injury Prevention and Control: Violence Prevention.
- Institute for Children and Poverty, The Hidden Migration: Why New York City Shelters are Overflowing with Families
- National Coalition Against Domestic Violence, Fact Sheets
- National Criminal Justice Reference Center, Family Violence - Facts and Figures

142   Local numbers aren't encouraging:

- In Oregon, 48% of victims remain in an abusive home because they do not have a safe and affordable place to live.

- 38% of all domestic survivors become homeless at some point. (http://www.voaor.org/Learn-About-our-Services/Children-and-Family-Services/Home-Free/Get-the-Facts-about-Domestic-Violence)

- Almost 50% of homeless women in San Diego, California, reported being victims of domestic violence (http://www.nlchp.org/content/pubs/Some%20Facts%20on%20Homeless%20and%20DV.pdf)

- Approximately 50% of families in the city's mainstream homeless shelter system in Washington, D.C., have experienced domestic violence.

- In Los Angeles, California, 34% of homeless family members reported being victims of domestic violence.

- In Kentucky, Tennessee, and the Carolinas, 60% of homeless parents living in shelters with their children reported experiencing domestic violence for a 2000 study.

- According to a 1999 report, 47% of homeless school-aged children and 29% of homeless children under five have witnessed domestic violence in their families.

143   http://www.nationalhomeless.org/factsheets/youth.html. Published by the National Coalition for the Homeless, June 2008.

144   http://www.nationalhomeless.org/factsheets/youth.html. Published by the National Coalition for the Homeless, June 2008.

145   http://www.nationalhomeless.org/factsheets/youth.html. Published by the National Coalition for the Homeless, June 2008.

146   http://www.destination-home.info/Homelessness/Data/national.htm#Special Populations and (National Alliance to End Homelessness, 2007. http://www.endhomelessness.org)

147   http://www.endhomelessness.org/pages/youth

148   http://www.nationalhomeless.org/factsheets/youth.html

149   http://www.nationalhomeless.org/factsheets/youth.html

150   http://www.nationalhomeless.org/factsheets/youth.html

151   http://www.nationalhomeless.org/factsheets/youth.html

152   http://www.nn4youth.org/crisis

153   http://www.nn4youth.org/crisis

154   http://www.nn4youth.org/crisis

155   http://www.nationalhomeless.org/factsheets/youth.html.

156   http://www.pbs.org/now/shows/526/homeless-facts.html

157   http://www.destination-home.info/veterans/vitalmission.htm#Contributing

158   http://www.destination-home.info/veterans/vitalmission.htm#Contributing

159   http://www.veteranscrisisline.net/ChatTermsOfService.aspx?account=Homeless%20Veterans%20Chat

160   http://www.hudhre.info/VeteransAssistance/

161   http://www.nationalhomeless.org/factsheets/Rural.pdf

162   http://www.nationalhomeless.org/factsheets/Rural.pdf

163   http://www.nationalhomeless.org/factsheets/Rural.pdf

164   http://seattletimes.com/html/nationworld/2009308417_apusruralhomelessness.html

165   http://www.nationalhomeless.org/factsheets/rural.html

166   http://www.nationalhomeless.org/factsheets/rural.html

167   http://homeless.samhsa.gov/resourcefiles/neqkwasx.pdf

168   http://www.pbs.org/now/shows/526/homeless-facts.html

169   http://www.pbs.org/now/shows/526/homeless-facts.html

170   http://homeless.samhsa.gov/Channel/Chronic-Homelessness-460.aspx

171   http://www.usich.gov/population/chronic

172   http://www.usich.gov/population/chronic

173   http://www.usich.gov/population/chronic

174   http://www.usich.gov/population/chronic

Appendix D - Websites & Organizations

175   http://www.heraldnet.com/article/20100923/NEWS01/709239891

ACKNOWLEDGMENTS

ACCESS
Alexandra Pauley
Ashland Police Department
Ashland DHS
Ashland Emergency Food Bank
Ashland Fitness & Tennis Club
Assia Awad
Barbara Mueller
Brenda Hall
Henry's Laundromat
Jahnna N. Malcolm
Janet Eastman
Jim Buser
Joe Borecki
Kickstarter.com
Lt. Mike Budreau, Medford Police Dept.
Maggie McLoughlin
Michael Reams
Mike & Trudy Coughlin
Norma Beecham
OregonAction.org
Oregon Center for Public Policy
Peter Fournier, Shower To The People
RVTD.org

And a very deep expression of gratitude to the former, car-dwelling homeless man from Los Angeles, who wouldn't share his name, but was incredibly generous to let me share some of his story. It was so similar to my own, but he told it so much better.

KICKSTARTER.COM PATRONS

This book would not have been possible without the generous support of the following backers on Kickstarter.com:

Assia Awad
Benjamin L Smith
Carol Lee Buck
Cassandra A. Loerke
Christine Alwardt
Cynthia Ceteras
Deanna DelRosso
Diane C. Paulson
Ernest Allred
Gary Einhorn
Glennie Feinsmith
Isha
Janet Eastman
Jesse House
J.K. Hermance
Jody Herriott
Joe Borecki
Joseph Linaschke
Kathleen Van Sandt
Kelly Martin
Kevin O. Lepard
Leonard S. Eshuis
Louis Mario Lipp
Maggie McLaughlin
Margaret (Peggy Price) Hartz
Maureen Wilson-Jarrard
M.L. Moore
Morgan C. Morningstar
Robert Gilmore
Sharry Teague
Steve Fenwick
Susanne McDonough
Theresa M. Johnston
Tiffany Lau
Virginia Nuzum
And thanks to one donor who wishes to remain anonymous.

ABOUT THE AUTHOR

My cat and I ended up living in my 30+ year old stationwagon with 400K miles on it, and no heater, because I lost my job and fell three months behind on rent. It was late Fall, and I hoped global warming would work in my favor with a mild winter. Unfortunately, the weather went the other way, and it got unseasonably cold, quickly.

I was on a waiting list for almost a month for an affordable storage unit, and less than a week before I became homeless, I got the call that one was available. In the cold and rain, I put my few belongings in my 5x5 space, and ended up with the flu and a fever for my efforts. I spent three days in bed fighting the illness, until I had no choice but to get up, sick as I was, and finish packing because I had to leave.

On move-out day, my next door neighbors, who were kind, generous, salt-of-the-earth people I really liked, saw me loading up my car with gear. They came over to say goodbye, gave me a card, and asked me if I had found a place to live.

"I'm staying with friends," I lied. In truth, none of my friends lived within 500 miles of me or had money to help me out, and none of my other efforts to secure a roof over my head had panned out. I wasn't surprised—who wants to house a perfect stranger with no money and no job?

My neighbors had enclosed $100 in the card, bless their hearts. I had a low two-figure monthly income, and that was all. I started car living with $230 to my name, and it was long gone within a month and a half.

Thanksgiving Day began at 4 a.m. with my cat puking and pooping all over every single blanket in use—he didn't miss one. With no laundromats open because of the holiday, I spent the freezing, foggy morning at an apartment building I used to live at, hosing down the blankets with ice cold water, and using the unlocked, outdoor, on-site laundry room to wash them cheaply ($2.50 total to wash and dry). My cat's stomach eventually settled down, and since the gym was closed for the holiday, we spent the cold but sunny day at my favorite park, which was mostly deserted.

The next day I had to go to a proper laundromat to wash the not-so-clean blankets again. While there, a former neighbor from the last apartment I'd lived in by myself came in to use the restroom. I hadn't seen her in three years, and she told me she had moved and bought a house with a cat door and a garden, not far from our former residences. I almost cried.

In early December, I took a skills test for a job I had applied for a month before becoming homeless. I passed with flying colors, and they scheduled me for an interview the week before Christmas. The day of the interview it snowed, so they called mid-morning and rescheduled for early January. By that afternoon, the sun was shining and the snow had completely melted.

The following morning I was in despair from the cancellation. I ran into a former landlord of mine at the gym, telling her how much I wished I could be back in the beautiful little studio I had rented from her. "Where are you staying now?" she asked. I told her I was living in my car. Without skipping a beat, she said, "Well, if you get a job, give me a call; if not, feel free to use me as a reference," and headed out to her yoga class. I wish I could say I was surprised, but I was used to that sort of response by then. People have to pretend they don't hear you, otherwise they'll have to get involved and do something. It's just so much easier to walk away, and assuage any guilt from doing so by thinking that your predicament must somehow be your fault. Or that it's due to some sort of moral failure on your part.

A couple hours later, I took my cat for a walk in one of the undeveloped fields near the gym, wondering how I would make it until the interview in early January. More snow was forecast, and the cold was becoming unbearable. I remember waking up at 2 a.m. a few days earlier and discovering my cat's water dish had frozen solid in the 27-degree weather. I went back into the gym, wondering if I'd ever see a warm bed and a roof over my head ever again. Then, while sitting at a table, working on the second draft of this book, two women approached me.

"Can we pay for a motel room for you for a month?" one of them asked. I looked up at her in disbelief. "No," I said, and then repeated it. "No." "Why not?" she asked.

I explained to her that I had already looked into every motel in the area that would accept pets, and a month's rent on an apartment would be far cheaper than any of them. Since it wasn't economically feasible, and it wouldn't solve my homelessness, it was crazy to spend that kind of money, only to end up back in the same situation a month later. She agreed, and introduced both herself and her friend, since I didn't recognize either of them from the gym. She and her husband walked their dogs every day in the same nearby fields where I took my cat, and I would often wave to them when they drove by. They would park and walk a quarter of a mile away from me, since they'd seen my cat panic at the sight of their dogs.

She told me she would lay awake at night, worrying about me, and that she'd come looking for me a couple times to no avail. I was dumbfounded. Since I had refused the motel, she then invited me to stay at her home instead, beginning later that evening. Even more stunned, I accepted.

In spite of the good fortune of a roof over my head and a warm bed, Christmas was very dark and depressing for me. While m y hosts and their family celebrated, my cat fell very ill with intestinal trouble (probably from the prolonged stress of car living). I spent Christmas Eve at the vet getting treatment for him, but she wouldn't listen to me when I told her what he needed. ("He's dehydrated and needs sub-q fluids." "No he's not.") He didn't respond to her treatment, and got much worse overnight. On Christmas Day, as he worsened further, I thought I would lose him and was utterly heartbroken. The vet bill had wiped out every last dime I had, and he was much worse off. Completely emotionally (and financially) exhausted, the next day I took him back to the vet and told her we were going to do things my way now. He got his sub-q fluids (and a couple other things), and improved rapidly. Not only that, but when I told the vet's staff that I was totally broke from the first bill, and couldn't pay the second one, they gave me a two-month payment plan. Merry Christmas, indeed.

My ever-generous host gave me a Christmas present of a gift card to a local grocery store, which helped pay for cat food and litter, which couldn't be bought with food stamps. She also gave me money for first month's rent in a roommate situation, once I interviewed for and landed the job that had been rescheduled for January (and whose delayed hiring process had helped keep me in my predicament). I offered to pay her back with my first paycheck. She refused and said it was a gift.

My new roommate's home was an old farmhouse on two acres less than two miles from my new job. He was happy to cede some pasture land to me to use for a garden to grow organic vegetables to donate to the local food banks, as I'd done the previous year. But my new job had very few hours to give me, so I started worrying about how I was going to pay the next month's rent. My new landlord said it was no problem, I could pay him whenever I got it, or over time if I needed to. I couldn't believe it.

A little over four months later, I went back to the undeveloped fields on the outskirts of town where I'd spent so much time while I lived in the car. I was looking for my cat's favorite scratching log to bring to him.

Strangely, it was gone. It had to have been taken recently, because I could see the imprint of its shape in the ground where I had le ft it. I walked around the fields looking for it to no avail, all the while remembering how many endless hours in the cold and wind and rain we'd spent out there. Other "landmarks" were still there, such as an overturned shopping cart in the middle of one field, and pine cat litter dust mulched neatly around the bases of shrubs and trees. I felt nothing.

As I got in the car, I remembered how my job search and an endless hiring process conspired to keep me trapped in my circumstances, and I started weeping. As I drove away, a male transient lugging a heavy duffel bag on his back was walking up the street toward where I'd just been. I pulled over to write these words in the parking lot of the nearby office complex where I'd slept most often. The lot was almost full, and one of the only open parking spaces was the same exact spot where I'd spent many a night.

Same place, same car, different day.

I continued to cry, because now I had the luxury to. Back then, I could only endure.

It's still too close. Too soon. Too painful. Because it could still happen again.